THE ADRIAN LIM
'RITUAL' CHILD KILLINGS

UNHOLY TRINITY

ALAN

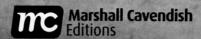

mc **Marshall Cavendish**
Editions

© 2016 Marshall Cavendish International (Asia) Private Limited

First published 1989 by Times Editions Pte Ltd

This 2016 edition published by Marshall Cavendish Editions
An imprint of Marshall Cavendish International
1 New Industrial Road, Singapore 536196

Designer: Benson Tan

Other Marshall Cavendish Offices:
Marshall Cavendish Corporation. 99 White Plains Road, Tarrytown NY 10591-9001, USA • Marshall Cavendish International (Thailand) Co Ltd. 253 Asoke, 12th Flr, Sukhumvit 21 Road, Klongtoey Nua, Wattana, Bangkok 10110, Thailand • Marshall Cavendish (Malaysia) Sdn Bhd, Times Subang, Lot 46, Subang Hi-Tech Industrial Park, Batu Tiga, 40000 Shah Alam, Selangor Darul Ehsan, Malaysia.

Marshall Cavendish is a trademark of Times Publishing Limited

National Library Board, Singapore Cataloguing-in-Publication Data
Names: John, Alan, 1953-
Title: Unholy trinity : the Adrian Lim 'ritual' child killings / Alan John.
Other titles: Adrian Lim 'ritual' child killings
Description: Singapore : Marshall Cavendish Editions, [2016] | [Second edition] | First published: Times Editions Pte Ltd, 1989.
Identifiers: OCN 934478206 | ISBN 978-981-47-5117-9
Subjects: LCSH: Murder--Singapore. | Trials (Murder)--Singapore. | Crime--Singapore. | Criminal--Singapore.
Classification: LCC HV6535.S55 | DDC 364.1523095957--dc23

Printed in Singapore by JCS Digital Solutions Pte Ltd

CONTENTS

A TRAGIC CAUTIONARY TALE

Thirty-five years have passed since two children were found dead within a fortnight in Singapore's Toa Payoh housing estate in early 1981. Agnes Ng Siew Heok was just nine years old, Ghazali Marzuki was ten. Their killers were arrested the day Ghazali's body was found, though nobody could imagine that day what police investigators were about to discover. Singapore has had some sensational murder cases but none has come close in terms of the bizarre revelations that emerged through the course of investigations into the so-called "ritual killings" and the trial of Adrian Lim, his wife Catherine Tan Mui Choo and mistress Hoe Kah Hong. Adrian Lim will be hard to beat as Singapore's most cruel, perverse charlatan and heartless killer. The case shone a light on a surprising reality of Singapore – that you do not have to scratch deep beneath the shiny surface of this clean, modern city state to discover age-old superstitions alive and thriving.

When Adrian Lim decided to pursue his interest in the occult and learn the practices of spirit mediums and traditional witchdoctors called *bomohs*, he landed in a goldmine that paid off handsomely. He found no shortage of desperate, naive and gullible people ready to place their faith in a self-styled guru chanting before an altar in his living room and ringing a bell. He called them his "devotees", and they parted with more than their money, jewellery and other valuables when they turned to him for help. He persuaded numerous teenage girls and young women that they would find everlasting happiness, good health, perpetual beauty and power over the men in their lives if they took off their clothes and had sex with him. Tan Mui Choo and Hoe Kah Hong were only two of those he tricked. The others included underaged students, bar waitresses and housewives, as well as well-off women complaining of headaches or insomnia, or wanting help to deal with sickness, unhappiness, wavering boyfriends and unfaithful husbands. If he lusted after a physically attractive young woman, he recommended repeat treatments of his altar rituals and regular sex with him. Some became his "holy wives" who stayed at his flat for extended periods; one "holy wife" became a prostitute at his urging and gave him thousands of dollars of her earnings.

Many of Adrian Lim's antics would be laughable if not for his extreme cruelty towards so many of his victims. Under the cover of being in a so-called trance, he acted out his depravity and subjected the women in his life to harsh physical abuse – beating, slapping and kicking them, pulling their hair and hitting their heads against the wall. Many were tortured with primitive and painful electric shock treatments he devised himself. During one such session, Benson Loh Ngak Hua, a young man married to Hoe Kah Hong, was electrocuted.

Adrian Lim's clients were persuaded of his powers when they saw him going into a trance before an array of statues and pictures of gods at his altar, professing devotion to a Thai sex god, an Indonesian Old Master and the Hindu goddess Kali. To convince a potential victim of his supernatural powers, he relied on a trick that never failed to leave people astonished and in awe of his abilities. Before a client's arrival he would insert blackened needles into an egg carefully. Then, during the ritual before his altar, he would chant and rub the egg over the person's body before breaking it open to reveal the needles. Everyone he duped this way was horrified by the sight, and he would claim dramatically that the needles were the evil he had removed magically from their bodies.

Adrian Lim's worst crimes of all were the senseless child killings that led to his arrest and that of Tan Mui Choo and Hoe Kah Hong. The unprecedented mix of murder, perverse sex, the occult and outright trickery proved unique in sparking widespread public interest in this case through most of the 1980s – from the day the unholy trinity were arrested in 1981, through their trial and the appeals of the two women, until the morning all three were hanged at Changi Prison in November 1988. Their court appearances drew hundreds of curious people who swarmed the surroundings of the Subordinate Court Complex and the Supreme Court building and waited for hours just for a glimpse of the three murderers.

This book gives a straightforward account of events following the arrest of Adrian Lim, Tan Mui Choo and Hoe Kah Hong. I relied mainly on the evidence produced at the High Court trial in 1983, including the long statements given to the police by the trio. I am grateful to the Registrar of the Supreme Court for providing access to the voluminous court records of the trial. Additional details are from the extensive newspaper reports of the two murders and the trial, especially in *The Straits Times*. The courtroom revelations needed little embellishment, because Adrian Lim, Tan Mui Choo and Hoe Kah Hong described all that happened in such graphic detail.

The Toa Payoh "ritual killings" of 1981 provided a larger-than-life warning to those too ready to seek supernatural shortcuts to dealing with the unhappy side of life. This book sounds a warning to those who despair over sickness, misery or relationships that sour and are prepared to seek a quick-fix solution from so-called miracle men claiming supernatural powers and rituals or potions that work. Adrian Lim was not the first self-styled healer to get into trouble with the law – and he was not the last. These days, Internet users go online to find help of exactly the sort Adrian Lim offered, and it appears readily available on websites that come complete with testimonials from satisfied customers. Sadly, some things never change.

Cruelty behind closed doors

Domestic violence is a theme that runs through the case of killer Adrian Lim. Behind closed doors, he was most cruel to the people closest to him. His wife and mistress were beaten repeatedly and tortured, and he exercised such total control over them that he made his wife become a prostitute and nightclub stripper, and got his mistress to bring him the child victims they murdered.

Too often, the perpetrators of domestic violence go unchecked because family members, neighbours and even some in positions of authority believe that when a man beats his wife or girlfriend, it is a private matter. I have been associated for some years now with Pave, Singapore's lead agency working with domestic violence and trying to change attitudes by spreading the message that violence has no place in any relationship, before or after marriage. Pave helps women and children who are victims or witnesses to domestic violence, and counsels men who are perpetrators of that violence. All the author's royalties from the 2016 edition of Unholy Trinity will go to Pave. To learn more about the agency and the work it does, please visit www.pave.org.sg

Alan John
January 2016

KEY PLAYERS IN THE TRIAL

The Murderers

The killers were arrested on 7 February 1981, hours after a second child was found dead within a fortnight near Adrian Lim's flat in Block 12, Lorong 7, Toa Payoh.

ADRIAN LIM: The 39-year-old was a married man who became interested in the supernatural and started practising as a spirit medium, attracting clients with various personal problems. He revealed to investigators the numerous tricks he used to demonstrate his supernatural powers and lure a steady stream of women into bed.

CATHERINE TAN MUI CHOO: Adrian Lim's 26-year-old second wife met him when she was 18 and moved into his Toa Payoh flat while his first wife and two children were still living there. He persuaded Mui Choo to become a prostitute and a nightclub stripper. She assisted at his altar rituals.

HOE KAH HONG: Adrian Lim's 25-year-old mistress was a married factory worker brought to him by her mother for treatment and she ended up becoming his "holy wife". She spent 45 days in a mental hospital after her husband Benson Loh Ngak Hua was electrocuted in Adrian's flat. Under Adrian's influence, she lured children to the flat.

The Victims

AGNES NG SIEW HEOK: The nine-year-old girl was at the Roman Catholic Church of the Risen Christ in Toa Payoh on 24 January 1981 when Hoe Kah Hong tricked her into going to Adrian Lim's flat. Her dead body was found stuffed in a bag left at Block 11, Lorong 7, Toa Payoh, early the next morning.

GHAZALI MARZUKI: The 10-year-old boy was spending the Chinese New Year holidays at his grandmother's Clementi flat when Hoe Kah Hong tricked him into accompanying her to Adrian Lim's flat on 6 February 1981. He was found dead outside Blocks 10 and 11, Lorong 7, Toa Payoh, the next morning.

BENSON LOH NGAK HUA ("AH HUA"): The 25-year-old jobless man died undergoing Adrian Lim's electric shock treatment on 7 January 1980. His wife, Hoe Kah Hong, told the inquest he was killed by a faulty fan, but the coroner recorded an open verdict, indicating that the circumstances of his death were unclear. After their arrests for the child killings, Adrian Lim and Tan Mui Choo were also charged with murdering Ah Hua.

CHRISTINA CHONG KIM HEW: She was an 18-year-old Malaysian student who became Adrian Lim's lover before he persuaded her to become a dance hostess and prostitute. From 1979 to 1981 she sent him almost $120,000 of her earnings, besides other gifts. Adrian returned $50,000 after his arrest and another $70,000 after the trial.

LUCY LAU: The young beautician went to Adrian Lim's flat to sell Tan Mui Choo beauty care products and cosmetics. Adrian claimed she became his "holy wife" and they had sex regularly. He was enraged when she accused him of rape in late 1980. The two children were killed soon after his arrest for rape.

The Investigators

INSPECTOR RICHARD PEREIRA: After Ghazali Marzuki's body was found, the detective followed a trail of blood to Adrian Lim's flat and met the killer who calmly let him inside. He recorded Adrian's 54-page statement that revealed bizarre tales of the occult, sex, violence and murder.

INSPECTOR SANMUGAM SUPPIAH: Better known as Simon Suppiah, he was overall in charge of the investigations into the child killings. He recorded statements from Tan Mui Choo and Hoe Kah Hong, who described graphic details of incest, unnatural sex, strange rituals, electric shock treatments and death in Adrian Lim's flat.

The Lawyers

GLENN KNIGHT, Deputy Public Prosecutor: He set out to prove that Adrian Lim, Tan Mui Choo and Hoe Kah Hong knew what they were doing when they killed Agnes and Ghazali. He was assisted by DPP Roy Neighbour. In his book *The Prosecutor* (Marshall Cavendish, 2012), Mr Knight said he ended up handling the Adrian Lim case when nobody at the Attorney-General's Chambers wanted to touch it because of the apparently ritualistic nature of the murders.

HOWARD CASHIN, counsel for Adrian Lim: He hoped to persuade the Court that Adrian was mentally sick with manic depressive illness and therefore not fully responsible for his actions. He was assisted by Mr Choo Han Teck. Mr Cashin, one of the most senior lawyers at the time, was assigned to represent Adrian and was paid by the government.

J. B. JEYARETNAM, counsel for Tan Mui Choo: He hoped the judges would agree that she had a mental illness, reactive depressive psychosis, and therefore not fully responsible for her actions. He was engaged to represent Mui Choo, who had money of her own. Adrian also agreed to give her $10,000 from the cash found at their flat for her legal fees.

NATHAN ISAAC, counsel for Hoe Kah Hong: His case was that she had a history of the mental illness schizophrenia and was suffering from it at the time of the child killings. He was assigned to defend Kah Hong.

The Trial Judges

JUSTICE T. S. SINNATHURAY: After a long career in the Singapore legal service, he was made a Supreme Court Judge in 1978. He was the lead judge at the trial and would frequently question witnesses himself. In his book *The Prosecutor*, Mr Knight said of Justice Sinnathuray: "He was an exciting judge to appear before. He had a very good mind but you could never be sure about how he would deal with the case. With most judges you could anticipate their train of thought, but with Justice Sinnathuray you couldn't. That was the challenging and exciting part of appearing before him."

JUSTICE F. A. CHUA: He was appointed a judge in 1957, making him the longest-serving member of the Supreme Court Bench in 1983 when the Adrian Lim case was heard.

CHAPTER 1

TWO MURDERS
AND A TRAIL OF BLOOD

The police had no leads after nine-year-old Agnes Ng Siew Heok was found dead in Toa Payoh in January 1981. Two weeks later, they were called to the scene of a second child killing, when 10-year-old Ghazali Marzuki's body was found. This time, bloodstains led detectives to Adrian Lim's flat.

For days now, Richard Pereira had thought of little else but Agnes Ng Siew Heok. There was little he wanted more than to find the killer who had murdered the nine-year-old and stuffed her body into a bag. Inspector Pereira, a detective with the Criminal Investigation Department's Special Investigation Section, had been asleep at home when he received the call, at about 3.30 a.m. that Sunday, informing him that a girl had been found dead in Toa Payoh. Intensive investigations followed as police combed the Toa Payoh area for anything at all that might get them on the killer's track.

But they drew a blank. There were no clues and no tip-off from anyone who might have seen something suspicious.

Agnes was found dead less than 24 hours after she disappeared. On Saturday, 24 January 1981, Agnes and her older sister Pauline, 13, left their flat in Block 233, Lorong 8, Toa Payoh, for their weekly religious classes at the Roman Catholic Church of the Risen Christ in the town centre. Agnes, a Primary Three pupil of Holy Innocents' Chinese Girls' School in Punggol Road, was the youngest of nine children. Her father was a Public Utilities Board wireman and her mother, a housewife. The girls arrived in church shortly before Agnes' class at 2 p.m. Pauline's class would end later, so Agnes was supposed to wait for her. But at 5 p.m., when Pauline was ready to go home, Agnes was nowhere to be found. She telephoned home and frantic family members began searching for the girl. When that failed, they reported to the Toa Payoh Police Station that Agnes was missing.

The little girl's body was found hours later, stuffed in a bag left outside a lift in Block 11, less than a kilometre from the church. The post-mortem showed death by asphyxia – something had been pressed against her face until she died. There were no injuries to suggest that Agnes had put up a fight. There were indications of sodomy and attempted vaginal penetration.

Parishioners attending Sunday services at the Church of the Risen Christ were stunned to learn about the child's death. Some who knew Agnes remembered her as a quiet, pleasant girl. Others recalled her bright, cheerful ways. Agnes' father told a newspaper reporter: "She was an obedient child and always listened to her elders." Pauline said: "I'm sure my sister knew her killer. She would never follow strangers or even talk to them."

In the days that followed, police officers and detectives questioned more than 250 people in Toa Payoh, especially those living near Block 11 and the church. They were hoping for just one clue which could lead them to Agnes' killer, but it eluded them. Then, on Saturday, 7 February, Ghazali Marzuki, a 10-year-old schoolboy, was found dead only metres from the spot where Agnes' body had been discovered. His bruised, bloodstained body lay sprawled under a tree between Blocks 10 and 11, Lorong 7, Toa Payoh. The post-mortem showed death by drowning and, like Agnes, Ghazali also appeared to have been suffocated. There was no sign of sexual assault but there were three burn marks on the boy's back and a puncture on his arm. Blood and tissue samples revealed the presence of a tranquilliser usually prescribed to adults who have trouble sleeping.

A Primary Four pupil of Henry Park Primary School, Ghazali was the youngest of three sons of a taxi driver and a housewife. On 4 February, he left the family's Holland Close flat to spend the long Chinese New Year weekend at his grandmother's home in Clementi. On the afternoon of 6 February, Ghazali and two of his cousins ate at a playground near their grandmother's block when a woman, dressed in blue and wearing sunglasses, approached them and asked if one of them would help her fetch something from a friend's house. One of Ghazali's cousins told the police: "She then asked Ghazali to accompany her, and he agreed. She led Ghazali by the hand and walked away with him." The boy got into a taxi with the woman and that was the last time he was seen alive. After his body was found, his distraught father told a reporter: "He was always obliging people and was a good, honest boy."

Many of the detectives who had been investigating Agnes' murder found themselves back in Toa Payoh early that Saturday morning, faced with a second child killing. Inspector Pereira was at his office in CID headquarters when the news reached him. He was at the scene within 25 minutes, just before Inspector Simon Suppiah, who was overall in charge of investigating the two murders, arrived. They found the body of a boy, dressed in shorts and T-shirt, lying face-up on the ground.

The two inspectors and their officers began searching the area and this time, they found a lead quickly. They spotted the first bloodstain between Blocks 10 and 11, then a second near a staircase at Block 12. Going up the stairs, they found a third bloodstain, then a fourth and a fifth. At the fifth level, Inspector Pereira and a police officer broke away from the others who continued up the stairs. The pair walked past flats along the corridor until they reached another staircase, and went up. At the landing between the fifth and sixth floors, Inspector Pereira found a bloodstain. He spotted another on the steps leading to the seventh level, but none beyond that.

He decided to check the flats on the seventh level. He stopped at the very first flat, 467F, and gazed at it for a while. There was a crucifix on the door and above the door hung a small oval mirror and a knife blade. A portly Chinese man standing along the corridor approached the detective and said he was the owner of the flat. Recalling the first time he set eyes on Adrian Lim, Inspector Pereira would later say in court: "I identified myself as a police officer and asked him his name. He told me that he was Adrian Lim and that he and his wife, Tan Mui Choo, were going to the Toa Payoh Police Station. He also told me that he had a girlfriend named Hoe Kah Hong, who was residing in Clementi but was also residing with him at the flat. I then asked him whether I could search the flat. He said that I could."

Adrian let Inspector Pereira into the three-room Housing Board flat. It had a rectangular living room with two bedrooms leading off on one side and, at the far end of the room, a passageway leading to the kitchen, bathroom and lavatory. The living room was a mess. The sofa and small tables were cluttered with newspapers, a cassette player, cassette tapes, books, the telephone directory, pillows, a torchlight, adhesive plaster, a pair of nail clippers, note pads and several plastic shopping bags. On the floral-patterned carpet were some thin mattresses and pillows and a blue plastic-topped table. At the far end of the living room, two crucifixes and a framed picture of the Sacred Heart of Jesus hung on the wall. There was an altar with several idols and photographs of various deities, and some of the photographs appeared to be smeared with blood. There was also a blood-smeared idol and a large Indonesian puppet whose moveable hands held a knife.

Inspector Pereira was struck by the eclectic mix of Hindu and Taoist idols alongside Catholic religious items and a statue of the Buddha. He thought it all very strange, but said nothing as he went into the kitchen. "I found what appeared to be a bloodstain in the kitchen area. I asked Adrian what it was. He told me it was red candle wax. But from my experience I was satisfied that it was a bloodstain," he recalled. The bloodstain, and Adrian's claim that it was candle wax, told the inspector this might well have been where Ghazali had been killed. He asked the officer with him to get Inspector Suppiah and the rest of the police party. It was now about 9.30 a.m.

Adrian did not stop Inspector Pereira from looking around the flat. A young woman arrived and when the inspector asked who she was, the woman handed him her identity card without saying a word. This was Hoe Kah Hong, Adrian's girlfriend, and she had come to tell Adrian that Tan Mui Choo was waiting for him at the bottom of the block. The inspector asked Kah Hong to get Mui Choo, and she left to do so. When Mui Choo arrived, the inspector asked her name and she too gave him her identity card. He recalled: "She did not speak at all. She just remained silent." She was unsmiling and appeared ill at ease.

Soon the flat was filled with policemen and detectives but Adrian, Mui Choo and Kah Hong appeared unperturbed.

Inspector Pereira flipped through a telephone directory and found a slip of paper with the name "Ng Siew Heok" written on it and some numbers. On a note pad next to the directory, in neat handwriting, he found: "Ghazali bin Marzuki, 10", a Holland Close address and a telephone number. The inspector learnt soon afterwards that the dead boy was Ghazali.

The bedroom at the front of the flat had a double bed, a single bed, a dressing table, a wardrobe and an easy chair. The second room also had a double bed, a dressing table and a wardrobe. Posters of the rock group Led Zeppelin hung on the wall. On the floor, a small altar placed on a sheet of cellophane held a religious statue, an oil lamp, an incense pot, a bowl with two eggs, and bottles filled with various fluids. There were bloodstains on the cellophane and on the headboard of the bed.

Inspector Suppiah was soon directing his men to photograph the altar, living room, bedrooms, bathroom and kitchen. Adrian remained in a bedroom with the two women, but then went up to Inspector Pereira to say he wished to explain something. He said Ghazali's name, address and phone number were written down when the boy came to the flat with a bleeding nose. Adrian said he treated the boy's nose, gave him $5 and the boy left. Adrian appeared calm all along, not at all bothered that several policemen were searching every corner of his flat. But his mood changed abruptly when officers from the Toa Payoh Police Station mentioned a rape charge. Now Adrian became angry and raised his voice. Kah Hong, who had been quiet all this time, became aggressive. She gesticulated and began to shout at the policemen.

Inspector Suppiah ordered his men to remove various items from the flat. These included bloodstained photographs of idols and the bloodstained Indonesian puppet idol. He also found a pair of bloodstained slippers near the television set. A handbag on the sofa contained a pair of lady's sunglasses. The police took that away, as well as the slip of paper with Agnes' name, the pad with Ghazali's name, and a plastic bag containing an electrical plug and wires. At 11.25 a.m., Inspector Suppiah told his men to take Adrian, Mui Choo and Kah Hong to CID headquarters. The flat was locked and a guard posted outside. Shortly after noon, the trio were in custody at the Special Investigation Section of the CID and the detectives prepared themselves for a long day of questioning their suspects.

By this time, word was fast spreading in Singapore that the two children found dead in Toa Payoh might have been victims of bizarre rituals involving human sacrifice, and that both had been mesmerised before being lured to their deaths. In Block 12, stunned neighbours now told of strange sounds they had heard from Adrian's flat. They recalled chanting, the ringing of bells and the sound of people jumping around. One resident said: "Suddenly after midnight we would be awakened by the chanting of mantras, just like you hear in temples. Then we would hear people jumping on the floor." Another said: "A few months ago, there were prayers and chanting in the flat. We reported to the area office of the Housing Board in Toa Payoh. The chanting stopped for a while and then started again."

But not even the most imaginative neighbourhood gossip could have guessed what tales of horror were unfolding at CID headquarters as Inspector Pereira and Inspector Suppiah got down to questioning Adrian, Mui Choo and Kah Hong.

CHAPTER 2

ADRIAN'S STORY: UNCLE WILLIE CHANGED MY LIFE

> He was married with two children and
> became fascinated with the occult and stories
> about men who possessed supernatural
> powers. In his statement to Inspector
> Richard Pereira, Adrian Lim said he paid for
> lessons before setting himself up as a fortune
> teller and spirit medium, and soon found it
> easy to trick women into having sex.

Adrian Lim was born on 6 January 1942, the son of a civil servant and a housewife. He was the eldest of three children and the family lived in middle-class Serangoon Gardens, a residential estate of narrow streets flanked by semi-detached and terrace houses. He attended Anglo-Chinese School until he failed the Secondary One examinations and dropped out. He said his first job, at 19, was as an Internal Security Department informant but he quit after a few months. His next job was with Rediffusion, the commercial broadcasting station. After three years as a wireman, he was promoted to bill collector and remained with the company for 14 years.

In 1964, when he was 22, he married his childhood sweetheart in a Roman Catholic church ceremony. They had a son and a daughter and, around 1970, bought a three-room flat in the new Toa Payoh Housing Board estate.

As a bill collector, Adrian was always on the move and met many people. He struck up numerous friendships, especially at a Katong coffeeshop he frequented. The conversation sometimes touched on the subject of the occult and *bomohs*, the traditional Malay practitioners of black magic. He was fascinated by the tales of men reputed to possess magical powers who could cast and remove spells, and help male clients win the affection of the women they desired. So when someone offered to introduce him to a practising *bomoh*, Adrian needed little persuasion. "I was inquisitive," he said in his statement, as he went on to describe how his life would change.

"Uncle Willie", the *bomoh*, lived in Upper Changi Road. His living room was like a temple, crowded with statues of Chinese and Indian deities. He had a wife and six children and they survived on gifts of cash from his clients. Uncle Willie told Adrian that people sought his help for all sorts of reasons. There were men who wanted to look handsome, women who wished to attract men, some asked him to cast spells on their enemies, and others sought love potions and magic oils. He showed Adrian his collection of Chinese, Indian, Indonesian and Thai idols and explained how they were useful in different ways. When Adrian expressed his interest in black magic, Uncle Willie offered to teach him. "He told me that the entrance fee was $360 and later, on each visit, any amount I wished to pay," he said.

Adrian returned to see Uncle Willie twice over the next two days. He said: "I remained in the house and observed Uncle Willie reading cards for people and from the replies of these people I believed he was very accurate in his analysis of their background, faults and character. I also observed people coming to his house and claiming to be possessed by evil spirits. After Uncle Willie chanted a few verses, he would give them some water to drink and they would seem to be all right. The act that finally convinced me that Uncle Willie possessed magical powers was when he went into a trance in front of the goddess Kali. There were about 100 people in the house on this occasion and I learnt that it was the birthday of the goddess Kali and the people were those who believed in her. Uncle Willie took a sword and started to cut his tongue and struck his body and back with the sharp end of the sword. I saw blood oozing out of his tongue after he cut it. He then started to spit blood onto the altar where the photograph of the goddess Kali and statues of other deities and gods were placed. The final act was the drinking of a bowl of blood which had been placed at the altar earlier. After he drank the blood, he came out of the trance."

Afterwards, Uncle Willie told Adrian he had felt no pain from the sword. Adrian handed over $360 and started his weekly lessons. "My first lesson was about a sex god of Siamese origin, Pragngan. I was taught some Siamese verses and the methods of using the god. The verses and use of the idol were supposed to heighten a woman's pleasure and desire for the man who recites the verses. Uncle Willie then showed me a bottle of concentrated rose perfume in a bottle placed in front of the sex god. He told me that the contents were prepared from an unmarried woman's bodily fluids and pubic hair, mixed with concentrated rose perfume. I was taught how to prepare it." The concoction was sold in small bottles to men who desired women, or women who wanted to make themselves attractive to men.

At his next lesson, Uncle Willie told Adrian that the sex god would "stay alive" if he set up an altar in his bedroom, made daily offerings of flowers and eggs and kept joss sticks burning continuously. When Adrian said he could not do any of that as his wife was a Catholic, Uncle Willie said the sex god could also be worn on his person. He gave Adrian a small statue of the sex god and told him to place it on an unwashed panty of an unmarried woman. Adrian was also told to get a soiled sanitary napkin of an unmarried woman, wrap it in a red cloth, and leave it at the sex god's altar. If possible, the idol should also be smeared regularly with the menstrual discharge of unmarried women. The four-hour lesson cost Adrian $90. "When I returned home, I placed the idol under my bed without my wife's knowledge. That night I had sexual relations with my wife and she appeared to enjoy it more than ever before. After that, I carried the idol with me whenever I left the house and when I wanted to have sex with my wife, I would place it under our bed."

In the weeks that followed, Uncle Willie showed Adrian how to administer a flower bath, by mixing flower petals into water to cleanse a person of bad luck. Adrian learnt about the different deities at Uncle Willie's altar and which to invoke for good luck or to have petitions answered. The most formidable of all, he was told, was the Hindu goddess Kali. "He told me that Kali was like a vampire and if she granted any request, the payment must be made in blood." Adrian said he was told that anyone who wished to worship Kali had to make an offering of blood. Also, to get her blessings, a worshipper had to drink human blood. Once a month, the Kali worshipper had to stand before her picture or statue, prick his finger and suck the blood. Chicken blood could also be used. "But to get the most from the goddess, blood from another person should be offered as a sacrifice. Uncle Willie did not tell me that I had to make human sacrifices to Kali."

Uncle Willie took Adrian to a North Bridge Road shop where he obtained supplies of concentrated rose perfume and small bottles in which to dispense his potions. Uncle Willie also taught him how to use the perfume, which had to be kept at the sex god's altar. "He told me that if I was going out, I should put some of the perfume on my eyebrows and, when attending dances, I was to put it on my neck. By doing this, I could easily attract girls and persuade them to be with me." Adrian paid $36 for a bottle.

At a Hindu temple in Serangoon Road, Uncle Willie pointed out the various deities and explained their powers. Adrian was taught the correct way to clasp his hands in prayer and was told he only had to utter the deity's name and speak his request. Any vow or promise he made to the deity had to be fulfilled once the petition or prayer was answered. Uncle Willie took Adrian to a Serangoon Road shop stocked with everything he would need to set up an altar of Hindu gods and goddesses. Adrian gave Uncle Willie a final payment of $200, but longed for one more lesson.

On a number of occasions, Adrian had seen Uncle Willie remove black needles from the bodies of his clients and observed that whenever that happened, the clients would be completely convinced of the *bomoh*'s powers. It took a lot of persuasion before Uncle Willie finally revealed to Adrian that this was just a clever deception and agreed to show him how to do it, provided he kept it secret. This was the needles-in-the-egg trick that Adrian would use to great effect when he set himself up as a spirit medium. Before a client arrived, Uncle Willie would take a few needles and burn them over a candle flame to blacken them. Using a pair of pliers, he would pick up the needles one at a time and insert them carefully into a raw egg, before sealing the puncture in the shell with powder. When the client arrived, Uncle Willie would chant as he passed the egg over the client's head or body. He would then place the egg before the goddess Kali at the altar and, after a few minutes, ask the client to break open the egg. Inevitably, the sight of the blackened needles would shock the client. Uncle Willie would immediately declare that the needles had come out of the client's body and were proof of a spell cast by an enemy. Grateful clients would either pay him or buy his perfumed potions. If the client was wealthy, Uncle Willie would say there were more needles still embedded in his body, requiring several more "extractions". This brought them back and he collected more money. Adrian said: "Although Uncle Willie showed me that the removing of needles from a person's body was a farce, I still believed that he had supernatural powers because I had seen him slash his body and his tongue with a sword but not suffer any serious injury. I asked him how he managed this feat, and he told me it was done with the assistance of the goddess Kali."

Adrian was now eager to learn more about Siamese gods and Malay black magic. Uncle Willie sent him to a man named Lee Tang Kee in Geylang. Adrian agreed to pay $500 for six weeks of lessons from Lee, who had a large altar of Siamese gods. "Lee Tang Kee taught me Buddhist prayers and incantations and Malay verses for casting spells and charms. He also pointed out the various Buddhist amulets, talismans and statues and explained the powers, taboos and prayers. Lee Tang Kee also told me that if I wanted my wife or girlfriend to stick with me, I should give them a glass of my urine to drink. Another method of making one's lover to stay forever is to make her suck your penis and swallow the sperm." Lee taught Adrian to read cards, giving him a chart listing the different meanings of the various symbols in a deck of playing cards.

Adrian continued working as a bill collector and kept up his interest in the occult by reading books on the subject. He had begun watching pornographic films at home and in

1973, police raided his flat and arrested him for possessing illegal movies. He was charged in court and fined. That left him feeling frustrated and while in this frame of mind, his bill collection rounds brought him to a house in the Alexandra Road area. The woman of the house was alone at home when he arrived. Susan was Chinese, married to a European oil rigger. Adrian struck up a conversation with her and discovered that she was part Thai. This got him talking and he found that Susan wore several Thai amulets. He told her about the occult and the things he had learnt.

After that visit, he would stop for a chat whenever he had to collect his Rediffusion payment. He learnt that Susan had several women visitors, most of whom were bargirls and dance hostesses. On one visit, Adrian offered to read Susan's fortune from a deck of cards. "It appeared that my reading was quite accurate because Susan was convinced of my powers. After I had Susan eating out of my hand, I asked her if I could rent a room to practise being a medium. She agreed. I was delighted because I could now put into use all the things taught to me by Uncle Willie and Lee Tang Kee. I grabbed the opportunity because I had paid a considerable sum of money for the lessons but could not practise the art at my own house." Susan asked for half his earnings plus $50.

Adrian went shopping in Serangoon Road for the photographs, idols and other things needed to set up his altar and stocked up on concentrated rose perfume from the North Bridge Road shop. Once the altar was ready, he was ready for business, and his first clients were Susan's mother and elderly women introduced to him by Susan. They came to have their fortunes read and Adrian sold them flowers for their baths. He told them flower baths would banish bad luck. He charged $5 for reading their cards and another $5 for the flowers. Soon he had a regular clientele of 10 women and he would head for Susan's house immediately after work. "After a few weeks, my wife started questioning me on my late hours as I used to come home after 9 p.m. I told her that I was collecting outstanding bills and she never questioned me again."

Soon the number of clients soared as Susan's bargirl friends also sought him out. He read their cards, sold them flowers and, for an extra $10, dispensed a small bottle of his rose concentrate. He told them the perfume would make them attractive to men. Adrian then discovered that some women were prepared to pay him and have sex with him too. "I came to know many girls, but only a few of them were fooled by me and submitted to intercourse. I picked the girl who was the most gullible and had the most problems."

The first was a Chinese bargirl and prostitute named Christina. She was about 22 years old and saw him for a month complaining of headaches. "After selling her amulets and potions and reading her cards, I managed to gain her confidence and she confided in me that she was a prostitute. From my observations, I gathered that she was the superstitious type and could be easily fooled by the use of religion and black magic. One day, she came to see me when there was no one around. She asked me to read her cards. I took this opportunity to tell her that her luck was bad and that she had no beauty to attract men and thus, was a failure as a prostitute. She asked me what could be done. I told her that if she dared to strip, something could be done. She agreed and took her clothes off.

"I took her to a rear room, bringing with me some rose petals and a small idol of the sex god. I made her lie on the bed in the nude and took off my clothes. She asked me why I was nude and I told her that it was part of the ritual. She accepted my explanation. I took the rose petals and rubbed them over her face. Later, I rubbed both her breasts with the rose petals and worked my way down to her vagina. After this, I discarded the rose petals and used the sex god. I moved the idol around her face and breasts. Later I placed it at her vagina and asked her to grip it with her thighs. After a while, I removed it and had intercourse with her.

"At first she objected, but I reassured her that in order to obtain spiritual beauty I had to have sexual intercourse with her as I was the guru and a holy person. Afterwards, I told her that she must come two more times and undergo the same thing before she would become attractive and earn money as a prostitute. I did not charge her for my services, but I told her to purchase some joss sticks and candles for the altar. I did the same thing to her when she came the next two times. After the third occasion, I told her that her business should improve. After that she used to visit me occasionally to buy the perfume. She told me that her business had improved and so I raised the price of the perfume from $10 to $15."

After this success, Adrian tricked other young women into having sex with him. Lorraine was a 16-year-old Indian girl who had trouble sleeping at night. Adrian persuaded her that sexual intercourse would give her beauty and peace. Linda was a 25-year-old Eurasian prostitute who complained of flagging business and customers who did not pay in full. Adrian prescribed perfume, flowers, amulets and sex with him. Margaret was a Chinese woman in her thirties, married to a senior hotel executive and the mother of two. She was unhappy because her husband was having an affair and she wanted him to return to her. After two consultations, Adrian told Margaret that she had bad luck and would not win back her husband unless she underwent three phases of a ritual in the nude. Margaret agreed. "Once she questioned me about the intercourse, but I told her that by having intercourse with me she had the advantage over her husband as I was a holy person."

In early 1974, 18-year-old Catherine Tan Mui Choo appeared. She was working in the Champagne Bar in Anson Road and came with two Eurasian bargirls, Anne and Liza. The three complained that some girls in the bar were jealous of their popularity and had cast a spell on them. They wanted protection. Adrian sold them his perfume and flowers, and asked them to return the next day for a more permanent treatment. When they came back, he took them into a room where they stripped. As he performed his flowers and sex god ritual, Adrian appraised their bodies. "I noticed that Anne's body was not good. Liza had a good body and Mui

Choo's was the best." He asked Liza and Mui Choo to return the next day, but told Anne the subsequent treatments were unsuitable for her as she had had a baby.

Liza and Mui Choo showed up as requested the next day. While Mui Choo waited, Adrian took Liza into a room and had sex with her, explaining that intercourse with him would purify her. He did not have sex with Mui Choo, although he performed the rose petals and sex god ritual and fondled her. He was sure that he wanted Mui Choo to be his mistress. On the next two occasions, he had sex only with Liza but told Mui Choo that he loved her.

Anne, Liza and Mui Choo came to him for weekly flower baths and as he gained Mui Choo's confidence, Adrian persisted in telling her that he loved her. "Once she told me that she could not have an affair with me as I was married. I told her that it was all right as long as my wife did not know about it. After much persuasion, I managed to get her phone number at her working place and contacted her often. I also went to the bar to meet her, and at times, to date her."

Adrian wooed Mui Choo. Each time she came to see him with her friends, he would take her into the back room where he fondled her. He believed she was a virgin. The first time they had sexual intercourse was at a flat in Pacific Mansions, off River Valley Road. After that, he would hire a room and take Mui Choo there for sex. She was convinced that he had supernatural powers because her business at the bar had improved since she met him. After a few months, Adrian told her he needed to have sex with her regularly because he had a heart ailment and her youth would help him to stay alive. "I think she believed me, because she became closer to me. I also believe that she looked up to me because she had a family problem and I was always present to give her advice and lend a sympathetic ear."

Mui Choo later quarrelled with her friend Anne, who advised her against having an affair with a married man. When Mui Choo told Adrian, he said she would have to choose between him and her friend. She chose to be with him. Mui Choo quit her job at the Champagne Bar, got a job at another bar and moved into a room at Dragon Mansion, near Spottiswoode Park. Adrian would visit her there and sometimes stay overnight. She began giving him money twice a week, between $100 and $300 at a time. When Adrian's wife questioned him about his nights away from home, he would lie that he had gone fishing overnight. He would even stop at the market on the way home and buy some fish. To allay his wife's suspicions, he gave her extra money and continued to have sex with her.

Adrian kept up his practice at Alexandra Road until early 1975, when his partner and landlady, Susan, quarrelled with him. She accused him of being too friendly with the younger girls and neglecting the older women. She also accused him of cheating her. "This was true, because while I was doing it she was just sitting around and collecting half of my earnings." He removed his altar from her house and stopped his sideline as a spirit medium and fortune-teller. In the middle of 1975, Mui Choo moved to Marine Parade.

Adrian, feeling the loss of earnings, now persuaded her to become a prostitute saying she would earn far more this way. Though reluctant at first, she eventually agreed. Adrian found her a pimp immediately and she entertained up to three men every afternoon, charging $150 each. The pimp got $50 per client and Adrian kept the rest. She continued to work in the bar at night.

One day Adrian took Mui Choo to his Toa Payoh home for his son's birthday party. He introduced her to his wife and said Mui Choo needed a place to stay. Afterwards, he told his wife that they could supplement his income by renting a room to Mui Choo. His wife objected and they quarrelled, but Adrian got his way and Mui Choo moved into the flat. To fool his wife, Adrian and Mui Choo would leave the flat separately and meet at a coffee house to wait for the pimp's calls. Adrian would return home after sending Mui Choo to the bar.

Nine days after Mui Choo moved in, Adrian's wife demanded to know if they were having an affair. When he denied it, she insisted that Mui Choo leave their home, but he refused to hear of it. They were shouting at each other, and his wife told him to choose between her and Mui Choo. His wife demanded that he swear before a picture of Jesus Christ that he was not having an affair. As he raised his hand to swear, he felt a sharp pain at his side. His screaming wife had tried to stab him with a kitchen knife. By now Mui Choo had emerged from her room and was watching them quarrel. Adrian's wife abused Mui Choo for breaking up the family, called her a whore and wailed that she wanted to die. At first Mui Choo denied everything, but suddenly she snapped and shouted back, telling Adrian's wife that if she wished to die, she should go ahead and kill herself. Mui Choo went to the kitchen, grabbed a container of tranquillisers and shoved them at the wife. Defiantly, the woman swallowed about 20 capsules. She was hysterical for a few more minutes before passing out.

Adrian telephoned his wife's parents and they arrived soon after. She was taken to hospital by ambulance. When his father-in-law began rebuking him, Adrian got fed up. He admitted that he was having an affair but attributed it to fate, and said there was nothing anyone could do about it. His in-laws took the two children and left. "Later that evening, I told Mui Choo that whatever happened between my wife and me, I would stick by her side and finally marry her. That night I had sexual intercourse with Mui Choo in her room."

His wife divorced him, citing Mui Choo as the co-respondent, and gained custody of the children. In early 1976 Adrian quit his job at Rediffusion and lived off Mui Choo's earnings from prostitution.

CHAPTER 3

TAN MUI CHOO: LIFE WITH ADRIAN

She was a teenage virgin working in a bar when she met Adrian Lim, and he seemed so nice. In her statements to the police, Catherine Tan Mui Choo described how the man she married got her to become a prostitute and nightclub stripper, persuaded her to have sex with her brother and beat her regularly.

Catherine Tan Mui Choo had experienced an unhappy, lonely young life. So when she found herself, at age 20, living with a man who was 14 years older and taking her earnings from prostitution, it still seemed better than what she had known before Adrian Lim. He spent time with her, spoke kindly, listened and was gentle with her. All this was more than she had received from any other man.

Mui Choo was the eldest of four children of a mechanic and a factory worker. From an early age, she felt that her parents, especially her father, did not want her. "My Dad was a very strict and serious man at home and I feared him. We never spoke to one another." As a child, she felt closest to her grandmother, with whom the family lived for several years. Her grandmother told her that she had been found in a dustbin. "When I asked what that was supposed to mean, she told me that my mother had wanted a baby boy. My mother did not want me." That made Mui Choo hate her mother. She felt that her parents preferred her two younger brothers and sister.

The family was Roman Catholic and Mui Choo was sent to the Convent of the Holy Infant Jesus in Victoria Street for her primary school education. She went on to MacPherson Secondary School and spent two years there before her father placed her, for no apparent reason, in the Marymount Vocational Centre, a residential home run by the Catholic Good Shepherd nuns for girls who were troubled, abandoned or from broken homes. "My Dad did not give me any reason. He just put me there. I did not like the centre because it was a place for runaway girls and I was not one of them. It made me feel that my dad really disliked me and did not love me." Her father visited her once a month, but her mother never came. After three years at Marymount, Mui Choo went home for Christmas and told her mother that she was not going back to the girls' home.

Mui Choo was now 16 and started working. She held a string of jobs, as a dentist's assistant, factory worker and clerk, earning between $120 and $400 a month and staying only a few months at each place. Her relationship with her parents did not improve, but she handed her pay to her mother. In 1972, Mui Choo lost her dearest family member when her grandmother died. She would visit the grave every Sunday morning and stay two to three hours each time. She left home the following year. "I found no happiness at home. Without Grandmother around, I was so lonely. Nobody cared for me, so I decided to be on my own."

She turned to Anne, an older Eurasian girl she had known from her Marymount days, who was working at the Seaman's Paradise Bar on Anson Road. Mui Choo accepted Anne's invitation to move in with her. Anne also suggested that she work in the bar. "She told me I could make more money. It was a kind of waitress's job, you just serve and sit down and talk to people. She even told me that she would keep an eye on me." Mui Choo worked briefly at the Seaman's Paradise before leaving with Anne for the nearby Champagne Bar. Her basic salary was $270 and she could earn another $400 each month in tips.

Mui Choo said she did not have sex with the men who patronised the bars where she worked. She only chatted and danced with them and went out to supper in Bugis Street with the other bargirls and their customers. She returned home twice or three times a month. Her father never spoke to her, and her mother did not care where she worked as long as she brought home some money. Mui Choo still felt lonely and unhappy although she was earning a considerable sum for a 19-year-old. One day Anne told her about a fortune-teller who might be able to help her, and took her to see Adrian at Alexandra Road. He spent half an hour reading her cards, and told her that her father was having an affair. "It made me hate my father more," she said. Adrian also said that her luck was very bad and would remain so unless she returned to him for nine flower bath rituals.

The next time Mui Choo went to see Adrian, she found several young women with him. He was chanting before an altar filled with statues of deities and decorated with flowers, and all the women were waiting for flower baths. When her turn came, Adrian told her to go to a bathroom and bathe with water from a tub in which flower petals were floating. Adrian then told her to go into a bedroom, strip naked and hold an idol in her hands as she sat. He went to the bedroom and sat before her, holding a rosebud. He chanted as he touched her all over her body with the flower. "I felt very embarrassed and uneasy, because it was the first time I had to strip in front of a man," she said. After the session, she dressed and went to the altar. "Adrian was very friendly. He talked a lot about his altar work and gave me the impression that he was really a holy man." Mui Choo went back for about five more flower baths.

One day a bargirl named Liza told Mui Choo that Adrian would sometimes insert an idol into the vagina of virgins who consulted him. This frightened Mui Choo and she confided in her roommate Anne, who telephoned Adrian at once to tell him. Adrian came to their flat and demanded to know who was spreading the "unfounded rumour". He summoned several of his women clients the next day. Liza was present, but she kissed his hand and denied telling Mui Choo any such thing. He then told Mui Choo to go before the altar and swear that she had told the truth, warning her that she would be struck by lightning if she lied. She also had to ring a bell nine times and light nine candles and nine joss sticks. Mui Choo swore that she had been truthful, but the other women said she was talking nonsense and took turns to kiss Adrian's hand. Mui Choo was left in tears.

A few days later, Adrian appeared at the Champagne Bar. And when Mui Choo got home that night, he was there. He chatted with her and persuaded her to continue with the flower bath treatment. He then invited her to meet him at a coffeehouse and she agreed because he had shown her that he was "a very nice and gentle man". Adrian asked Mui Choo about her family and listened intently as she described her unhappy home life. "He talked to me very nicely and gave me the impression that he had a very caring attitude towards me. He sympathised with me for having to work in the bar and because my family didn't want me. He even asked about my working place, and if anyone bullied me, and he was ready, you know, to kind of look after me, the way he talked to me. I looked up to him like a big brother because he had a very caring and warm attitude towards me." They spent two hours together and Adrian did most of the talking, but she did not mind. No one had ever been so good to her.

After that, Adrian called every night to ask how she was doing. They also started meeting regularly. He told her that he had a weak heart and was a dying man. He said a Chinese physician had told him that young girls like her could help his ailment. When he broached the subject of sex, Mui Choo was embarrassed. She was still a virgin. Adrian reassured her that if she was afraid of intercourse, they could have "bodily contact only". She eventually agreed and he took her to a room in Pacific Mansions where "he made love to me without sex". They returned there several more times and, one day, had sexual intercourse. "He told me I could save him as he was a dying man and I believed him. I felt sorry for him." She said she never enjoyed the sex act. Adrian told Mui Choo later that she alone could not save his life and asked her to bring her younger sister to Pacific Mansions. She did as he requested. Adrian took the 15-year-old schoolgirl into a bedroom and Mui Choo waited outside. The girl emerged weeping, but said Adrian did not do anything to her.

More changes were to occur in Mui Choo's life. She moved to a room in Dragon Mansion and started work at another bar. Adrian visited her every week and they had sex regularly. He complained that his wife was cruel to him and this also made Mui Choo feel sorry for him. But she also recalled: "All this while, deep in my heart, I was wondering what I was doing with a married man. On occasion, I wanted to sever the relationship with him, but I was unable to speak out." Adrian now began suggesting that she should become a prostitute, and said he needed to go to Europe for heart surgery. Mui Choo resisted the idea initially but relented after moving to Marine Parade. Adrian took care of finding the clients and on her first day, she had sex with two men. When she contracted a venereal disease, Adrian took her to a doctor and looked after her for a month until she recovered.

Adrian began encouraging her to move into his Toa Payoh flat, but Mui Choo resisted because she did not like the idea of being with his wife and two children. He was at her flat one day when his demeanor changed suddenly. "He was so violent, beating his chest and shaking his head, and he was saying in a low voice, in Malay, why am I so stubborn, am I trying to cause him to die when he has a weak heart. This frightened me." Afterwards Adrian told her he had been in a trance, and said she should obey him because his "holy people" knew what was best for her. Mui Choo then agreed to move into his Toa Payoh flat. Within days of her arrival, his wife and children were gone.

Adrian now busied himself setting up an altar in the living room of the flat. One day, he appeared to go into a trance and, speaking in an unfamiliar voice, told Mui Choo that he was the "Old Master". He told her she had to swear obedience to him before the altar, ring the bell nine times while holding nine joss sticks, and if she broke her word, she would break her head.

Mui Choo did as instructed, although she was not sure at the time whether to believe it. Still in a trance, Adrian informed her that she was now his "holy wife". He said there were three gods who could "breeze in and out of his body". They were the Old Master, Datuk Pragngan and Adrian's soul, named Ah Liah or "Long Time No See". If Mui Choo was at all sceptical about Adrian's supernatural powers, his trances and the spirits that were able to enter and possess his body, he soon provided her another reason to obey him: he assaulted her. The first time he beat her, it was because she did not want to take some antibiotics prescribed by the doctor. Another time, he beat her because his "holy people" told him she did not entertain her male customers well enough. Once he attacked her as soon as she returned from having sex with a client. "He pulled my hair and gave me a few hard slaps." Adrian claimed to be in a trance every time he beat her.

Having quit his job as a bill collector, Adrian now settled into his new role as a spirit medium. He lit joss sticks at his altar and pricked his finger to rub blood on the picture of the goddess Kali. People started coming to have their fortunes told and they began calling him Guru. Then, sometime in 1976, several months after she had moved in with Adrian, there was yet another change in Mui Choo's life.

"Out of the blue he suddenly wanted me to go into show business and told me he would teach me how to dance." Adrian was inspired by the amount of money nightclub artistes reputedly earned. From watching various nightclub acts, he was confident that he and Mui Choo could be just as good; he would dance and she would strip. They practised their act and soon they were performing in nightclubs in Singapore and Malaysia. Whenever they had stints in Singapore, Adrian worked as medium during the day and on their days off, and Mui Choo continued to be a prostitute.

The beatings continued, about three or four times a month. If she sulked after a beating, he would strike her again. If she pulled a long face because she did not like her work as a prostitute and stripper, he beat her. If she lost her temper, he beat her. "Sometimes, he pulled my hair, slapped me hard and tore my clothes and kicked my legs." Adrian also attacked her in front of his clients, and told them that he treated Mui Choo like a devotee and she deserved to be punished if she did anything wrong. "After each beating, my ears would ring and then my cheeks would swell as if I had mumps. Sometimes I had blue-black marks on my cheeks and thighs," she said, but she never sought help or saw a doctor.

The people who came to seek Adrian's help included those with marriage problems, men and women having trouble with their girlfriends or boyfriends, and bargirls wanting flower baths and blessings. He drew on a host of tricks to meet every need. When a client arrived, he would read the person's fortune in the cards. At the same time, he would size up the client to determine how well off the person was. If an item of jewellery attracted him, he would declare that the future looked dim and the particular gold ring or pendant would only make things worse. Invariably, the client would leave the item behind. Adrian would go into a trance and tell his client what the god wanted – usually sums of $90 or more. He also sold medicines. Those who complained of having difficulty sleeping were given tranquilisers, not knowing that they could get the same at any clinic. Some were sold holy powder to place in their homes to ward off evil spirits. He started calling his clients his devotees, and they were also asked to donate towards the birthday celebrations of various deities.

The performance that never failed to convince those who came to the flat was the needles-in-the-egg trick Adrian had learnt from the *bomoh* Uncle Willie. Mui Choo said Adrian saved this for people he declared possessed. He would say an exorcism was required and instruct the person to return on another day, and to bring some eggs for the ritual. Before the appointment, he would prepare an egg filled with blackened needles. When the client arrived, Adrian would place the client's offering of eggs at the altar and begin chanting. In the midst of chanting, he would discreetly place the egg with needles among the others. He would stop chanting and invite the client to break open the eggs. Sometimes, Adrian would take the egg and rub it all over the client's body before breaking it himself. The sight of the blackened needles falling out of the cracked egg never failed to evoke astonishment, fear and awe, and convinced people that Adrian had supernatural powers. He would announce that the evil had been successfully removed and collect an appropriate donation.

In June 1977, Adrian married Mui Choo at the Singapore Registry of Marriages but there was no settling down. They carried on with their nightclub jobs; he continued his increasingly lucrative sideline as a medium and she was a daytime prostitute.

One day Adrian told Mui Choo that she would remain young and beautiful forever if she had sex with young men and swallowed their semen. He told her the sex god required this of women who believed in him. The first was a teenager named Shafie, who used to come to the flat regularly for supplies of perfume for his mother, a *bomoh*. Adrian told the boy that the sex god had willed that he should have sex with Mui Choo. Shafie agreed immediately and Adrian watched as the boy had sex with Mui Choo. This went on for about six months. Later, Adrian persuaded Mui Choo's younger brother, a 16-year-old, to have sex with her. Mui Choo overcame her initial reluctance and had sex with her brother regularly for about a year.

Adrian continued to say he needed young girls for his ailing heart and over the next three years, numerous women who went to the flat had sex with him. While in a trance, he declared them all his "holy wives". Mui Choo would wait outside the bedroom while her husband had sex with a woman. Sometimes she left the flat before a "holy wife" arrived and Adrian would tell her to call before returning.

Shortly after their marriage, Adrian and Mui Choo met Christina Chong Kim Hew, an 18-year-old secretarial student from Kuala Lumpur. She came to the Toa Payoh flat with a man they had met while performing in a Kuala Lumpur nightclub. During that brief visit, Adrian read Christina's cards, went into a trance and told her she was possessed by the devil and had needles in her head. To convince her, he performed the needles-in-the-egg trick. "Before she left, I told her that she was fated to be Adrian's mistress and that if she wanted to remain young and pretty, she had to sleep with him," said Mui Choo. Christina returned a week later and stayed three months, during which she occupied the master bedroom with Adrian and Mui Choo slept in the second room. Adrian gradually persuaded Christina to become a prostitute and to send him the money she earned. "Adrian started by asking her for a couple of hundred dollars, but at one stage, she was sending him $6,000 to $7,000 a month," said Mui Choo. Christina continued sending money up to the time of the child murders in 1981.

Sometime in 1979, a woman brought her mentally ill adult daughter to see Adrian. Hoe Lai Ho had been hospitalised at Woodbridge Hospital, the government-run mental hospital, but her condition did not seem to improve. Adrian said the young woman would have to stay at his flat for a month for treatment. He decided that she required his electrical treatment, which he had been experimenting with for some months on Mui Choo and Christina. He made Lai Ho and Mui Choo sit on two chairs with their hands interlocked and their feet in a plastic tub filled with water. Adrian then placed a live wire in the water as he placed his electrical device on their heads. Both women trembled as the electricity passed through their bodies.

Lai Ho was groggy after the treatment. Adrian took her into a room, gave her three tranquillisers and was soon undressing her for sexual intercourse. When her mother came later to check on the progress of the treatment, Adrian performed the needles-in-the-egg trick. Mui Choo said the mother was "astonished and extremely happy as she felt that the evil spirits had come out" of her daughter. The electrical treatments and sexual intercourse continued for the rest of the month. Adrian then declared the treatment complete and said Lai Ho could go home. The mother was so pleased that she brought another daughter, Kah Hong, to Adrian. Kah Hong's problems were that she could never agree with her mother, suffered head pains and was very hot-tempered.

CHAPTER 4

HOE KAH HONG: ELECTRIC SHOCK TORTURE AND TRAGEDY

> Hoe Kah Hong said in her statement to the police that she became Adrian Lim's "holy wife", endured his electric shock treatments and was coached to hide the truth after her husband Ah Hua was electrocuted. Weeks before the child killings, she found Adrian upset and angry at being accused of rape.

On 7 January 1980, a year before the child killings, the police were called to Adrian Lim's flat. Benson Loh Ngak Hua, 25, lay dead in a bedroom, next to an electric fan. Known as Ah Hua, he was legally married to Hoe Kah Hong, but they had not yet held their customary Chinese wedding with the tea ceremony and banquet. He died while spending the night at the flat.

Kah Hong told the police and the coroner's inquiry that followed that they had been in bed when Ah Hua felt hot and was electrocuted when he got up to switch on the fan.

The coroner recorded an open verdict, indicating that the circumstances of his death were not entirely clear. What escaped detection was that although Ah Hua had indeed been electrocuted, he had died while undergoing Adrian's electric shock treatment. Adrian had told Mui Choo and Kah Hong what to say to the police and ordered them to clean the flat and get rid of all evidence before the police arrived. He told Kah Hong to put up a convincing show of grief when Ah Hua's parents came and she howled when they arrived. Mui Choo wept too.

Ah Hua died about three months after Kah Hong, 25, had been brought to Adrian by her mother for treatment. She was the third in a family of six children. Her father died when she was eight, and whenever her mother could not cope, Kah Hong was sent to live with an aunt in Penang. She had a year or two of primary education in Singapore and went to school briefly in Penang. She returned to her family in Singapore when she was 15. She helped her mother run a school canteen stall and held a couple of other jobs before she joined Hewlett Packard as a factory worker. She remained with the electronics company until her arrest.

Kah Hong met Ah Hua in 1974 or 1975, while on an outing to the Chinese Garden in Jurong with a group of friends. He tried to date her, but she turned him down because she regarded him as a casual friend. He persisted, bought her a surprise present for her twentieth birthday and continued asking her out. Her mother disapproved because he was unemployed. "However, he kept on wooing me for two to three years and I finally brought him to my house. When my mother met him, she took a liking to him and gave me her consent to go out with him," Kah Hong said. They registered their marriage when they were about 22 years old. They had saved enough for their Chinese wedding ceremony when he died.

Kah Hong was happy at home and at work until her elder sister Lai Ho became mentally ill and would get jealous if Kah Hong got along well with their younger sister. Lai Ho had been mentally ill since being jilted by a boyfriend, and their mother took Lai Ho to various temple mediums seeking treatment. Lai Ho also became jealous when Kah Hong started dating Ah Hua. "Sometimes, for no rhyme or reason, she would give me a slap. She scolded me in the presence of her friends and I could not tolerate it," said Kah Hong. She also felt that her mother favoured Lai Ho and this made her angry. She began disliking her mother and would lose her temper easily. "I banged things, I would ignore my mother when I saw her. I thought of leaving the house and on one occasion, I packed my clothing and wanted to go, but my brother scolded me and slapped me." Although she stayed, she still flared up easily and would ignore the others in the family, or throw her clothes at her mother or sister in a fit of anger.

One day in late 1979, Kah Hong's mother took her and her younger sister to Adrian's flat, telling them they were going to a temple to pray. Lai Ho had been staying at the flat, undergoing treatment. Adrian told them about his Old Master, who entered his body when he was in a trance. He said that he was supposed to have gone abroad on nightclub engagements, but the Old Master had commanded him to remain in Singapore. If he disobeyed, the Old Master would make him hit his head until he died. Adrian then made Kah Hong and her younger sister take turns to sit before him, look into his eyes, think of Buddha and chant some verses after him. "I thought he was a god. He said his eyes were swollen from crying. I thought so too," Kah Hong recalled. Adrian then turned away and sat cross-legged, facing his altar. He took a lemon and began slicing it. A slice flew up and landed near Kah Hong. Adrian said that was a sign that there were evil spirits in her. She believed him and was frightened. She was even more impressed when he performed the needles-in-the-egg trick on Lai Ho.

Adrian pronounced Lai Ho cured but almost immediately drew a card from a playing pack and declared that Kah Hong was possessed by an evil spirit. She was shocked. Her first thought was that Ah Hua must have cast a spell on her because she liked him less than he liked her. Adrian gave Kah Hong's mother a tranquilliser which made her sleep, and stayed up a long time talking to Kah Hong, giving her advice on ways to avoid bad luck and quarrels. He asked her about herself, her family and Ah Hua. They spoke until 2 a.m., by which Kah Hong was convinced that Adrian was a good man and a disciple of Buddha. He remained in a trance throughout. He also told Kah Hong that he had a weak heart and did not have long to live. When Mui Choo patted him on his forehead, called his name, and pressed his elbows, he appeared to snap out of the trance and he asked: "What time is it? Why is it so late?"

The second time Kah Hong visited Adrian's flat, it was Mui Choo who seemed to be in a trance, wearing a sarong and holding a snake near the altar. Adrian told Kah Hong to sit in front of Mui Choo as she chanted, held up the snake's head and swayed. Kah Hong stared at the snake, felt nauseated and vomited. Her younger sister, who was there too, also vomited. Mui Choo then told Kah Hong that her dead father's spirit was in her. Adrian joined in to say that when her father was alive, he had fooled around with women. To drive out her dead father's evil spirit, Adrian said, Kah Hong would have to accompany him into a bedroom. She was made to sit on the floor with her feet in a tub of water and he covered her head. "Suddenly I trembled all over and saw lights everywhere although my head was covered with a black cloth. This, I later learnt, was the electric shock treatment. Afterwards, Adrian told me that my face was not as it had been before. He said I looked prettier."

A few days later, Mui Choo telephoned Kah Hong and asked several questions about herself and her family. Mui Choo told Kah Hong that Ah Hua had an eye for other women and if she did not believe this, she should bring a photograph of him to the flat. One evening soon after, Kah Hong went to the flat alone. "Mui Choo was painting her fingernails. Mui Choo said I was not my father's child. She said my mother had an affair with someone else and gave birth to me. That was why I did not look like my sisters." Kah Hong believed this and, angry to hear that she was illegitimate, blurted that her mother had warned her not to trust Adrian and Mui Choo completely. Mui Choo told Adrian that it was in fact Kah Hong's mother who had cast a spell on her own daughter. Adrian ordered Kah Hong to drink her own urine to drive out the evil spirit in her. She obeyed, but this was apparently not good enough and he told her to drink some of his urine. She did so. Then he produced two coins, placed them in her mouth and flipped them in the air. One landed tails-up, the other, heads-up. "He said that proved that I was charmed by my mother and I believed him."

Mui Choo then took Kah Hong into a room, stripped her and examined her body "to see if there was any evil" and snipped off some of Kah Hong's pubic hair with a pair of scissors. Mui Choo reported to Adrian that Kah Hong's flesh was firm. Kah Hong stayed with them and in the days that followed, Adrian and Mui Choo told her repeatedly that her parents and Ah Hua had cast evil spells on her. While in a trance, Adrian warned her that once she started living with Ah Hua after their Chinese wedding ceremony, he would drive her into prostitution. Adrian said Ah Hua was already living off the earnings of dance hostesses and had a mistress in Johor Bahru. This did not strike Kah Hong as absurd because Ah Hua was unemployed. "I cried. I asked myself why my mother, my father and my husband were trying to harm me." She was in this state of depression when Adrian told her she was not fated to be with Ah Hua and should marry him instead.

After Mui Choo assured her that this was the right thing

to do, Kah Hong became Adrian's "holy wife" in a ceremony before the altar. Adrian stayed in a trance throughout, speaking in a low voice and only in Malay. With her hands tied to his, Kah Hong bowed before his altar and rang a bell. Adrian pronounced them "married in heaven" and, still speaking in Malay, informed his newest "holy wife" that they would now have to do what all married people did – have sex.

Adrian slept with Kah Hong that night, but they did not have intercourse until the next afternoon, while Mui Choo was out. "I did not like the act and remained like a piece of wood. Adrian did not like it and told me that I was like wood," she said. He made her watch some pornographic movies before taking her back into the bedroom, where he taught her how to perform oral sex. He taught her various sex techniques which he said were approved by the sex god, Datuk Pragngan. She learnt to enjoy sex with Adrian, who told her that during the act, his power would pass over to her. He sodomised Kah Hong and also made her swallow his semen, telling her it was holy because he was a holy man. He declared her "a fast learner".

Adrian kept up his efforts to turn Kah Hong against her mother and suggested several times that she should hit her mother with a broom. He also told her to go home and collect her clothes, jewellery and bank passbook. "I collected all my belongings and was about to leave when my brothers and sisters tried to stop me. I flew into a rage and fought with them. I also smashed the idols at the family altar," said Kah Hong. During the commotion, someone called the police. Ah Hua was there too, and he told the police that he was her husband and she was leaving home. When her mother went to Adrian's flat later to persuade her to return home, Kah Hong struck her with a broom. Her mother returned with Kah Hong's two brothers, but she beat them too, and they fled. Her mother tried coming again, but this time, Kah Hong and Mui Choo attacked the woman and poured urine over her head.

Then Ah Hua came looking for Kah Hong. Adrian told him that she needed treatment and there was no reason to worry because she was in safe hands. He also invited Ah Hua to visit whenever he liked, and to stay with them too. Ah Hua began spending weekends at the flat. It was now late 1979 and the date for Ah Hua and Kah Hong's customary marriage was approaching. On the weekends when Ah Hua stayed over, Adrian made him sleep in the same room as Kah Hong, but she said they did not have sex. Adrian had told her to be nice to Ah Hua, but she now hated him because she believed he was living off the earnings of prostitutes. When Ah Hua was present, Adrian did not have sex with Kah Hong. Instead, he gave the couple his electric shock treatment. Ah Hua's father visited the flat and had the electric shock treatment too, after Adrian told him he had an evil spirit in him. "He received the shock treatment until he could not take it and begged for mercy," said Kah Hong.

Ah Hua had been spending weekends there for about two months when he came on 6 January 1980 with the invitation cards for their wedding banquet. He had dinner with Adrian, Mui Choo and Kah Hong, and afterwards the four of them sat together, talking and laughing. Kah Hong then recalled that Adrian once told her that if Ah Hua really loved her, he would let her place her panty and soiled sanitary napkin on his head. She decided to test him but when she placed the panty and pad on his head, he flung them off and got angry.

Adrian then said it was time for the electric shock treatment. Kah Hong agreed and persuaded Ah Hua to join her, but he was afraid. Adrian coaxed him, saying it was an evil spirit in him which made Kah Hong indifferent towards him. Ah Hua finally relented and Adrian decided he would administer the electric shock treatment to Kah Hong and Ah Hua simultaneously. He made them sit on the floor with their feet bound in a tub of water. Using a syringe, he pumped urine up their nostrils, making both vomit. Adrian put a small brass idol in Ah Hua's mouth and placed a chain around his neck. Despite Ah Hua's protests, Adrian placed one of Mui Choo's panties and a soiled sanitary napkin on his head, telling him this was necessary to mock the devil. Adrian told Ah Hua and Kah Hong to lock their arms as a sign of marriage and he covered their faces with cloth.

"All of a sudden I lost consciousness," Kah Hong recalled. "When I came to, I sat on the sofa while Adrian and his wife tried to wake my husband, Ah Hua. They were unable to revive him." Adrian told her that Ah Hua was dead, and explained that the evil spirit in her body had jumped out and killed him. The two women panicked, but Adrian remained calm and told them what to do. They removed the tub, cleaned the flat and dragged the body to the room Ah Hua usually shared with Kah Hong. Before calling Ah Hua's parents and the police,

Adrian told Kah Hong what to say when they arrived. She would say that at about 4 a.m. Ah Hua woke up complaining that he was feeling warm. He asked her to get the fan but when she refused, he went to get it himself. A loud sound suddenly woke her and she found the room in darkness. Then she saw Ah Hua on the floor, with the plug of the fan near his hand. Once Kah Hong memorised her lines, they called the dead man's parents and the police. The cover-up worked, but this was not their only brush with the law that year.

In late 1980, Adrian was arrested and charged with rape. The complainant was Lucy Lau, a young cosmetics salesgirl who came to the flat to show Mui Choo how to use various beauty and skin care products. Adrian was at home when Lucy arrived and after the product demonstration, the three of them went to dinner at the Mandarin Hotel's Chatterbox Coffeehouse. They got on well together and Adrian invited Lucy to join them and some friends on a nightclub outing the following weekend. She agreed and after that, they became quite friendly.

One day in October 1980, Lucy asked Adrian to read her cards, telling him that she had been troubled ever since her grandmother's death. Adrian told her that her grandmother's spirit was disturbing her and the only remedy was sex with him. Mui Choo took Lucy into a bedroom, stripped her and checked her body. Adrian then gave Lucy a tranquilliser mixed in milk and as soon as she dozed off, he took her into the bedroom and had intercourse and anal sex with her. He left her lying naked on the bed and joined Mui Choo in the kitchen. When Lucy woke up and realised what had happened, she was in tears, but Adrian told her it was fated that she should have sex with him.

Adrian and Mui Choo said he had sex with Lucy on another four occasions. Then, in early November, Lucy's parents came to the flat and asked to borrow $3,000. When Adrian handed Lucy's father $700 and requested an IOU note, he became furious but promised to return the money in a few days. Three days later, Mui Choo called Adrian from Lucy's home and told him to come right away. When he got there, Lucy's father demanded to know what Adrian had done to his daughter, but Adrian denied any wrongdoing. Two men then appeared and began punching Adrian and hitting him with a stool. The police arrived next, and Lucy accused Adrian of having raped her. Adrian was sent to hospital to be treated for his injuries. That very night he went to the Toa Payoh Police Station to report that he had been assaulted, only to find Lucy and her parents filing a rape report against him. He was arrested and charged. Adrian cried when he got home. Two days later, Mui Choo was arrested and charged with helping him to commit rape. Both were allowed bail and had to report to the police station fortnightly to renew their bail. Adrian asked Kah Hong to help him by telling the police that she was at the flat on every occasion that Lucy visited and there had been no rape.

The rape report upset Adrian a great deal, but Mui Choo and Kah Hong stood by him. It was already late 1980 and the unholy trinity was only weeks from committing more heinous crimes.

CHAPTER 5

AWAITING TRIAL

It took two years before the trial of Adrian Lim, Tan Mui Choo and Hoe Kah Hong began in the High Court. The time lag did nothing to diminish public interest in what was now dubbed the "ritual killings" case.

On 9 February 1981, two days after their arrest, Adrian Lim, Tan Mui Choo and Hoe Kah Hong were charged in court with murdering Agnes Ng Siew Heok and Ghazali Marzuki.

When the case was mentioned again a week later, all the spectators' seats in the courtroom were filled and hundreds of people waited in the grounds of the Subordinate Courts complex in Havelock Road, eager for a glimpse of the accused. It was clear that this would be no ordinary murder trial. The horror of the crimes, the child victims, the religious objects found in the Toa Payoh flat and speculation that these might have been ritual killings stirred anticipation of bizarre revelations in court. The large crowds would turn up each time Adrian, Mui Choo and Kah Hong had a date in court. All three were ordered to undergo a month's psychiatric observation at Changi Prison Hospital.

On 7 April 1981, Adrian and Mui Choo were charged with murdering Kah Hong's husband, Loh Ngak Hua. Magistrate Aziz Yatim said the psychiatric reports showed that all three were fit to stand trial for the child killings.

The preliminary inquiry into the child killings was heard before magistrate Chang Kok Ming on 16 and 17 September that year. Mui Choo was represented by lawyer and opposition politician Mr J.B. Jeyaretnam, and Kah Hong by Mr Nathan Isaac. Both women denied the charges, but Adrian, who still had no lawyer, pleaded guilty and told the magistrate: "I am the one who engineered and planned the whole killing. I plead guilty for the record to save everybody's time. The women are not to be blamed. They are under my control."

DPP Glenn Knight called 58 witnesses and produced 185 exhibits, including 104 colour photographs taken by police at the murder scenes and inside Adrian's flat. There were also playing cards, tranquillisers, an array of religious idols, medical syringes, a book entitled *Witches, Wraiths and Warlocks*, and a newspaper clipping headlined "Human Lives Offered to Placate Gods".

The magistrate ordered all three to stand trial in the High Court. Adrian told the magistrate at the end of the hearing: "I have to thank you and all the ladies and gentlemen." Told that he would have to supply a list of witnesses if he wished to call any, he said: "Well, I think that I am the best. I do not have [any witnesses]. I am the best ... I am the main one."

The three remained behind bars for 18 months more before their trial began in the High Court on 25 March 1983. More than two years had passed since the children were found dead, but interest was quickly rekindled in what had come to be called the "ritual killings" case. The story made headlines not only in Singapore but also in regional newspapers and news magazines. The trial lasted eight weeks, making it the second-longest murder trial in Singapore's legal history after the Pulau Senang trial of the 1960s, when 18 criminal detainees were jointly tried, found guilty and sentenced to hang for committing murder on the former penal island.

Mr Knight had the task of proving the case against Adrian, Mui Choo and Kah Hong without any eyewitnesses. "But it will be my case that the circumstantial evidence is far more damning than any eyewitness account can ever be," he told Justice T. S. Sinnathuray and Justice F. A. Chua at the start of the trial. Mr Knight was assisted by DPP Roy Neighbour.

Adrian now had a lawyer, Mr Howard Cashin. Mui Choo was represented by Mr Jeyaretnam and Kah Hong by Mr Isaac.

Adrian and Mui Choo were also charged with the murder of Kah Hong's husband Ah Hua, but the prosecution proceeded only on the child killing charges. Adrian and Mui Choo pleaded guilty as charged, but the judges rejected their plea because in a murder trial, the prosecution must prove its case. If found guilty of murder, Adrian, Mui Choo and Kah Hong faced death by hanging. The lawyers for all three indicated that they would not be challenging the facts produced by the prosecution, but hoped to use psychiatric evidence to persuade the court not to impose the death penalty.

CHAPTER 6

PROSECUTION: "THEY INTENDED TO KILL"

Adrian Lim's trances, rituals and sexual appetite may have attracted most interest, but Deputy Public Prosecutor Glenn Knight said the crux of the case before the court was whether Adrian Lim, Tan Mui Choo and Hoe Kah Hong meant to suffocate and drown their child victims. He was confident of proving this beyond all reasonable doubt.

Glenn Knight had one main task to perform at the trial of Adrian Lim, Tan Mui Choo and Kah Hong Kah Hong: he had to cut through a jungle of dramatic, bizarre and seemingly inexplicable revelations and prove that the three accused meant to kill Agnes Ng Siew Hock and Ghazali Marzuki and pursued their aim to tragic ends.

Opening his case in Courtroom 4 of the Supreme Court, the Deputy Public Prosecutor said although there was evidence of "unholy ritualistic practices" at the Toa Payoh flat, he did not have to rely on all that to prove his case. The acts of murder were committed independently of those various practices. "That kind of evidence would go towards explaining possible motives for killing these children. But we are not required to prove motive under our law of murder," he said. "Whether these three persons, when they abducted and killed these children, were actuated by a need to indulge in ritualistic evil practices or were actuated by a need to satisfy the unnatural sexual desires of one or more of them, matter not for proof of guilt of murder. What matters is that they did intentionally suffocate and drown these two innocent children, causing their deaths in circumstances which amount to murder. And this we will prove beyond all reasonable doubt."

Mr Knight said the prosecution would establish that the two children were taken by deception or force and remained in the hands of the three accused until they were killed. At the very least, he said, the accused intended to suffocate and drown the children. They did this intentionally and it was sufficient in the ordinary course of nature to cause death. Under Singapore's laws, this was murder. The evidence, taken as a whole, would overwhelmingly prove that Adrian, Mui Choo and Kah Hong intended more harm on the two children than inflicting mere injury. "They intended to kill," he said.

Agnes had been sexually assaulted and suffocated to death. She was last seen alive at about 4 p.m. on 24 January 1981 by her sister Pauline at the Church of the Risen Christ.

She was found dead early the next morning. "The anguish caused by Agnes' death was compounded by a telephone call her mother received on January 31. It will be our case that either Mui Choo or Kah Hong made that call. In that call, the mother was told that the caller was a good friend of Agnes and that she had better watch out for her other daughter, Pauline. She was told that the caller would recognise her and would chop her up." Ghazali was found dead on 7 February 1981, a day after Kah Hong approached him and his two cousins near their grandmother's Clementi home. Ghazali had been suffocated and drowned.

Mr Knight told the court that police detectives who searched Adrian's flat found Ghazali's telephone number and the names of his two cousins written on a note pad in the living room. They also found a slip of paper, with Agnes' name and telephone number. A pair of bloodstained slippers was found in the hall. A pair of shorts and a handkerchief, both stained with Group B blood, were found under a table in the living room. They were Adrian's. Idols and pictures of Indian deities at Adrian's altar were smeared with blood. A small altar placed on a sheet of cellophane in one of the bedrooms had a Group B bloodstain. Police found numerous drugs in the flat, including the tranquilliser found in Ghazali's blood. Strands of hair like his were found under a carpet and under the sofa in the living room. In a pail, they found Kah Hong's bloodstained blouse. A syringe containing Group B blood was also found. The police found various electrical gadgets, books on witchcraft and a newspaper cutting about human sacrifice. They took away a total of $159,340, in $1,000, $500, $100 and $50 bills, kept in the living room.

Among the early witnesses was Changi prison doctor Gandhi Muthu, who had examined Mui Choo and Kah Hong on a number of occasions after their arrest. He said Mui Choo had told him about the electric shock treatments and he found small areas of discolouration on her soles where Adrian applied the electricity. Dr Muthu also found patches of hair loss on her head and scars on her thighs. Although he could not say conclusively if the scars were caused by electric shocks, he said he did not rule out the possibility. Kah Hong also had small areas of hair loss and multiple areas of discolouration on her lower back, but he could not say if these were caused by electric shocks.

Consultant forensic pathologist Wee Keng Poh, who performed the autopsies on both children, said Agnes was suffocated and Ghazali was drowned. The injuries he found on Agnes' eyeballs, lungs, lips and tongue were consistent with something – a hand, for example – being placed over her nostrils and mouth to prevent her from breathing. There were no neck injuries, which excluded the possibility that she was strangled with a string. He said it was possible that a pillow was pressed to her face to suffocate her. Dr Wee said Agnes was also sexually assaulted. He said it was possible that Ghazali may have been suffocated and drowned, but the immediate cause of death was drowning as the boy's lungs were waterlogged. Small bruises on the head suggested that Ghazali's face had been pressed against a hard surface. The injuries were consistent with his head having been pushed into a tub of water and pressed down. Dr Wee found a single puncture wound on the boy's lower right arm. It was a fresh wound, so it was possible that something was injected into his body or blood had been drawn out. Bruises on the boy's legs could have been caused by tight gripping. There were three greyish-black burn marks on Ghazali's back, caused after death and traces of a sedative in his blood, stomach, liver and skin tissue. The drug, not usually prescribed for children, was probably given to Ghazali before he died.

Adrian's lawyer, Mr Howard Cashin, asked if there were any injuries on the children's necks to suggest that they had been dealt karate-style blows. Dr Wee said karate chops could have been delivered to the heads of the children, because there was blood under their scalps. Questioned by Mr J.B. Jeyaretnam, Mui Choo's lawyer, Dr Wee said it was easier to drown a person who had been drugged as the person would struggle less. To a question from Kah Hong's lawyer, Mr Nathan Isaac, Dr Wee said it was not possible to tell whether the burn marks on Ghazali's back had been caused by a heated object or electricity.

On Day Two of the trial, Toa Payoh resident Fung Joon Yong told the court that at about 1.10 a.m. on 7 February 1981, he was using the public telephone at the bottom of Block 12 when two of his neighbours, Adrian and Mui Choo, walked past. Mui Choo was carrying a dark complexioned boy over her shoulder. Mr Fung, a welder, had been living in the block for 12 years and his flat was two floors below

Adrian's. He knew that Adrian originally lived there with his wife and two children and that Mui Choo moved in later.

Mr Isaac suggested that Mr Fung had identified Mui Choo wrongly as the woman carrying Ghazali because it was in fact his client, Kah Hong, who carried the body. But Mr Fung stuck by his story. Mr Fung said he knew something of Adrian's family life from listening to his mother and neighbours, and denied that members of his family went to Adrian's flat to worship idols. He said the neighbours talked about the worshipping going on in Adrian's flat but added: "I didn't hear any noises from his flat, but other neighbours mentioned that they heard noises."

Re-examined by Mr Knight, Mr Fung maintained that it was Mui Choo, not Kah Hong, whom he had seen carrying the boy. Asked if he could identify the man with her that night, Mr Fung pointed at Adrian, who stood up in the dock and grinned. Mr Fung grinned back. He was about to leave the witness box when Mr Isaac asked what he had around his neck. He removed a string of amulets and held them up for all to see. There was laughter in the court. Asked if he had got them from Adrian, Mr Fung said he had not and added that Adrian's amulets "could not fight" the ones he wore. Asked what he meant by that, Mr Fung replied that he was only joking and denied that he had worn them to court to protect himself from Adrian.

CHAPTER 7

INSPECTOR SIMON SUPPIAH: MORE CONFESSIONS

Few who were eager to know what lay behind the Toa Payoh child killings of 1981 could have been prepared for what was to unfold as the trial of Adrian Lim, Tan Mui Choo and Hoe Kah Hong entered its second week and Detective Inspector Simon Suppiah, the man in charge of investigations, revealed what the accused told the police.

Inspector Simon Suppiah spent two days in the witness stand going over with DPP Glenn Knight three signed statements by Adrian Lim, Tan Mui Choo and Hoe Kah Hong after their arrest. The statements described their roles in the child killings, with some inconsistencies in each of their accounts. He also provided a long list of the items the police removed from the Toa Payoh flat in the days that followed the arrests.

Kah Hong's lawyer, Mr Nathan Isaac, was cross-examining him when Inspector Suppiah revealed that the police had recorded three more extensive statements from each of the accused. He spent much of his third day in the witness box reading out Kah Hong's 23-page statement and parts of Adrian's 54-page statement. Mui Choo's statement was 31 pages long. These statements, as well as two more by Adrian and Mui Choo concerning the death of Kah Hong's husband, Loh Ngak Hua, were admitted as evidence. Mr Knight told the court that these five new statements did not figure in the prosecution case and were actually part of the defence case.

Three girls who escaped

The longer statements recorded by Inspector Suppiah and Inspector Richard Pereira exposed the ghastly specifics of the life led by Adrian, Mui Choo and Kah Hong in the years leading up to the child killings.

The court heard accounts of unnatural sex, blood-drinking, supernatural practices, and trickery, and learnt that Agnes and Ghazali were not the first children lured to Adrian's flat. Kah Hong said that three young girls she brought to the flat escaped with their lives because Adrian found them "unsuitable". Kah Hong told Inspector Suppiah that after Lucy Lau's rape report, Adrian was furious with the police and got the idea to kill young children after having sex with them. "He added that all the deities and gods at the altar had agreed to his killing the young children. He then instructed that I get three young children while his wife got three children. I agreed," she said.

Kah Hong said she was at her room in Clementi when Adrian telephoned one day in December 1980 and told her to get the "fish" – their code for children. She looked around in Clementi before going to Toa Payoh Central, where she spotted three Indian children – two boys and a girl. She went up to them and asked if one of them could help her fetch some books from a friend's flat. One of the boys volunteered, but she said she preferred the girl to accompany her. Kah Hong took the girl by taxi to Adrian's block and before going up to the flat, she telephoned from the ground floor to say that she had brought a "fish". Adrian and Mui Choo were watching television when Kah Hong arrived with the girl. Adrian scrutinised the child but rejected her, saying she was too big. He also told Kah Hong that he did not want an Indian child because that might offend the goddess Kali. The girl was given $2 and Kah Hong sent her back to Toa Payoh Central.

A day or two later, Adrian telephoned again and asked Kah Hong to bring him a child. She was tired after her day at work, but she went out that evening and looked in the Clementi Avenue 2 area. She spotted a group of children playing in a field, went up to them and asked if one of them would go with her to a friend's house to collect some cosmetics. Pei Ling, a girl aged about 10, agreed to go with her and they took a taxi to Toa Payoh. This time, Adrian rejected the girl on sight, saying she was so small-built that he might injure his penis if he tried having sex with her. The girl remained in the flat for about half an hour before Adrian, Mui Choo and Kah Hong took her back to Clementi by taxi.

After this second failure, Adrian told Kah Hong to bring him a child who had "some flesh". She said: "He also told me that I should get the child at about 6 p.m., when my appearance would be like that of a ghost, which would have the power to lure the child. As instructed, I left the house at about 6 p.m. and went in search of the victim at Clementi Avenue 2." She spotted two Chinese girls near a shop, went up to them and used her usual line of asking for help to fetch some things. One of the girls, Alice, agreed to go with her and they took a taxi to Toa Payoh. Adrian and Mui Choo were not home when they arrived, but Kah Hong had her own key. At first Alice refused to enter the flat, but Kah Hong persuaded her and gave her some chocolate. Adrian and Mui Choo returned at about 8 p.m. This time Adrian approved of the child and asked Kah Hong to give her some sedatives. Alice swallowed only two of the three capsules offered her, and before they could take effect, she began insisting that she wanted to go home. She then picked up the telephone, called a friend and told her friend that she was in Toa Payoh. When she put down the telephone, Alice announced that her mother knew where she was because her friend told her mother that she had been taken away by a Chinese woman. "On hearing this, Adrian panicked and told me to send Alice home," said Kah Hong.

Adrian Lim's devotion to Kali

Inspector Richard Pereira took a week to interview Adrian and record his 54-page statement, an autobiographical account of his life, moving from his family history and childhood to his first marriage, his interest in pornographic films, his lessons in the occult with Uncle Willie and Lee Tang Kee, and his life with Mui Choo and Kah Hong. Summing up his beliefs and activities, Adrian said: "I am an ardent believer of the goddess Kali. I believe in her powers and will do anything to gain her blessings. I do not possess any supernatural powers but, through the needles-in-the-egg trick, have managed to convince my wife and others of my supernatural powers. The powers of the sex god are also false and I used that to have sexual intercourse with anyone and with my wife's consent. All those whom I had sex with were actually raped by me as I had frightened them through the use of falsehoods and trickery. I preyed on their weaknesses and superstitions and made them take empty oaths and vows in the presence of idols and deities. My wife was one of such victims."

Adrian described how he set up his practice as a spirit medium at his flat after his first wife and two children moved out, and his reputation grew as time went by. He said that apart from selling flowers, holy perfume for the sex god and talismans, he also dispensed tranquillisers to those who complained they were unable to sleep. From about 1976, he started seeing two doctors at their Whampoa clinics and obtained from them a steady supply of various drugs, especially tranquillisers. Sometimes, Mui Choo or Kah Hong would collect the medicines for him. One of the doctors also extracted blood from Adrian, Mui Choo and others for Adrian's altar rituals. Adrian said he told the doctor he performed voodoo acts at home and also worshipped a Hindu goddess whose devotees were expected to drink human blood. "He extracted blood from Mui Choo and myself and emptied the syringes into separate bottles. We paid him $10 for his services. I placed the bottles of blood in the fridge at home. When it was midnight I would take the bottle out from the fridge, dip my finger into both bottles and smear the blood on the pictures of the Goddess Kali. After this I would light joss sticks and drink the blood in front of the altar. Mui Choo would do likewise." Later, Mui Choo took several young women to the doctor to have their blood extracted too. A Malay woman *bomoh* who bought perfume from Adrian introduced the "blood donors". Adrian smeared their blood on the pictures of the goddess, and he and Mui Choo also drank the blood.

After he had set up the altar in his flat, Adrian said he resumed seeing Uncle Willie. On one of these visits he met an Indian gravedigger named Samy, a fervent Kali devotee. Adrian visited Samy at his house one day and saw him go into a trance before the picture of the goddess Kali. While in that state, Samy took a razor blade and cut his arm without causing serious injury. Later, at Uncle Willie's house, Adrian noticed some metal skewers near the altar and asked what they were for. Uncle Willie said he pierced his cheeks and tongue with the skewers while praying to Kali. "He then demonstrated the piercing to me and I noticed that there was no blood. Later Uncle Willie told me that if I wanted to do it, I must ask Kali to help me do it. I sincerely believed that if I were to be devoted to Kali, I could do the same things as Samy and Uncle Willie."

Adrian and Mui Choo were now also nightclub performers. He decided to pep up their act by including a sequence during which he pierced himself with skewers. "I did as I was told by Samy and Uncle Willie, that is, I prayed to the Goddess Kali. I then pierced the skewer through my cheeks. It was quite painful at first, but surprisingly there was no blood. I bore the pain and carried on piercing the skin at my throat and both my arms. I did not stop or yell because I knew that by doing this, my act would be in great demand as it was one of a kind in Singapore and Malaysia. Furthermore, it injected a new interest in my act as stripping was getting a bit monotonous."

Sometime in 1977, Adrian and Mui Choo were performing in a Kuala Lumpur nightclub when he befriended a Malaysian named Sunny Low. Adrian told his new friend that he was a medium who knew a lot about Thai black magic, including the sex god, and knew how to cast spells and grant protection to those who came to him. Later that year, Sunny came to Singapore and spent an evening at Adrian's Toa Payoh flat. He wanted a bottle of the sex god perfume. He also brought a teenager named Christina Chong Kim Hew.

Adrian wanted to have sex with young women and he knew that Mui Choo loved him a lot and would do whatever he asked. "Furthermore, she believed I had supernatural powers and was superstitious. I drummed it into her that whatever the gods requested me to do I could not forsake them and had to carry out their wishes to the letter. I then devised a scheme with her. I told her I would make her a sort of assistant and it would be her duty to physically check all young girls whom I had a desire for. We both agreed on a silent code to signal whether a girl's body was good enough for me to have intercourse with. The first victim was Christina Chong."

About three weeks after her first visit, Christina appeared at the flat alone one day and told Adrian that she had been given away for adoption at an early age and never knew her real parents. She said she had left her adoptive parents' Malacca home but suffered severe headaches and believed that her adoptive parents had cast a spell on her. "When Christina came to my house and told me her problems, I thought of a way to convince her that I was really a medium and had supernatural powers. I then remembered the needles-in-the-egg trick Uncle Willie had taught me a few years back. I read her cards and told her that her mother had sent 'flying needles' which were embedded in her head and body. Christina then asked me to see in the cards whether she could pursue a career as a secretary as she was taking a secretarial course. As I had further plans for her, I told her that she would not be a success as a secretary and that she must lead a carefree life," said Adrian.

Christina asked him to remove the "flying needles" in her body, so Adrian told Mui Choo to take the girl into the bedroom and check her body. Mui Choo understood that she should see if the young woman was suitable for sex.

While the women were in the room, Adrian went to the kitchen and inserted five needles into an egg the way Uncle Willie had shown him. He then placed the egg among nine others at his altar. When Mui Choo brought Christina out of the room, she touched the side of her head to signal that the teenager had a good body. Adrian then sat cross-legged before his altar, a saffron cloth draped over his shoulders, and began to recite some Thai verses he had copied from his former teacher Lee Tang Kee.

"After reciting some prayers and chanting I asked Christina to take one of the eggs in the plate. I knew which egg contained the five needles. The first egg Christina took did not contain the needles. I then asked her to break it into a bowl after passing the egg over her face and head. When she broke it and there was no needle, I told her that there was a hard fight between my powers and those of the flying needles. She took a second egg and after passing it over her face and head, broke it into the bowl. Again there were no needles. This time I told her that the needles had been embedded in her body over a long period and it was quite difficult to get them out.

"I then offered her the remaining eight eggs and invited her to pick one. This time she picked the egg with the five needles. After passing the egg over her face and head, I made expressions on my face and groaned to show the difficulty. In actual fact it was a show as I knew the third egg contained the needles. After that I gave her the egg and asked her to break it into the bowl. When she broke it, she saw the five needles and immediately she was convinced of my powers. My own wife, who was unaware that I had placed the needles in the egg myself, was also astonished. I did not tell her that I was the one who did it." He told Christina that he had removed all the needles her mother had embedded in her body.

He added: "I did not tell my wife about the egg trick because if she was convinced of my powers it would be easier for me to use her and make her do my bidding without any questions asked. In short, I would get absolute obedience."

Adrian persuaded Christina to stay at the flat, become his "holy wife" and have sex with him. At his bidding, she quit her studies, became a prostitute and sent him a substantial part of her earnings. Recalling the night he first had sex with Christina, Adrian said he told her that he could give her eternal beauty. "I told her there were three phases in the ritual whereby a person obtained spiritual beauty and the protection of the sex god. I told her that she would have to lie in the nude while I, also in the nude, passed some rose petals over her face, breasts and vagina, followed by the second phase where I pass the sex god over her face, breasts and vagina and place the idol at her vagina and make her grip it with her thighs. I also told her that I, being holy, had to have intercourse with her to pass some of my powers into her body. After I told her all this, she agreed. I then got her into her room while Mui Choo remained in the hall. I went through the first and second phases of the so-called ritual. Then I took a pair of scissors and cut her pubic hair. When she questioned me, I told her this signified cleanliness.

"I made love to her and then licked her vagina until she could not bear it any more. After this I had sexual intercourse with her. After discharging, I rested by her side and kept on making love to her. After a few minutes I used some KY lubricant and applied some of it on her anus and on my penis. At first she rejected it as being unnatural. However, I managed to convince her that it was part of the ritual and if all phases were not completed, the spiritual power would be weak. When she submitted, I inserted my penis into her anus. Initially she complained that it was quite painful but I kept reassuring her until I discharged in her anus. After that, both of us slept in the back room in the nude until the following morning."

It was while Christina was at the flat that Adrian devised his electric shock treatment, initially as a means of curing her persistent headaches. He bought a coil of electrical wire, a plug and two connector plugs. He knew something about electrical connections from his old job as a Rediffusion wireman. He linked the connector plugs to the plug in such a way that only the electricity from the positive points were bare at the connector plugs. Adrian told Christina that by passing an electrical charge through her, he would cure her headaches. When she was reluctant to try it, he turned on the device and applied it to his own head. "I felt a sensation running down my body. There was some pain, but it was like ant bites." Adrian told her that evil spirits feared electricity and knives. He took two chairs and placed them on either side of a plastic tub filled with water. He then told Christina and Mui Choo to strip to their underwear and sit on the chairs with their feet in the water. He took four kitchen knives and made the women grip a knife under each armpit. He also made each woman grip a pair of scissors in the folds of her stomach. As the women locked their hands, Adrian placed a live wire into the water.

"I noticed that both of them were trembling. I then took the connector plugs and placed one on the left temple of Catherine and the other on the right temple of Christina. They trembled violently. I left the plugs on their temples for about 10 seconds. Before I finished counting to 10, both of them screamed. I then removed the connector plugs from their temples. I was shocked to see hair from their heads sticking to the connector plugs. After they had settled down, I went through the same procedure again but this time only for about five seconds or so. This time, too, they screamed with pain. After the process was over, I gave them each a glass of urine which I had earlier prepared. I did this because I was taught by Lee Tang Kee that a woman who consumes a man's urine would remain with him forever. After they had consumed the urine I checked their temples and noticed some burn marks." Mui Choo took some tranquillisers and went to bed. Adrian took Christina into the back room and had sex with her.

Adrian also described some of the other women in his life. He used his persuasive powers, combining his sad story about his ailing heart with his apparently supernatural powers, to get young women into bed with him.

There was Mui Choo's younger sister, who was still in school when Adrian convinced her that she was destined to have sex with him. Over a six-month period, he had sex with her regularly and convinced her that she should become a dance hostess and prostitute. She started working at a brothel by day and at a nightclub at night, handing over all her earnings from prostitution to him. He also persuaded her to have sex with her brother and Shafie, the *bomoh*'s son with whom Mui Choo had also had sex. She stayed at the Toa Payoh flat for about a year before she was arrested in a vice raid and placed in a girls' home.

Ani was a Malay girl he invited home after she complained that of being molested by her guardian's husband. She stayed for 10 months. Susie was a young clerk to whom Adrian prescribed weekly sex for nine weeks. She paid him $1,500 for his services and an amulet. On the ninth occasion that Susie came to the flat, Christina Chong came too. "After having sex with Susie in the back room, I told her that Christina had also come to have sex with me. This annoyed her a lot. I said this because she was quite old and I wanted to get rid of her. After this last occasion, Susie never came to my house again." Alice was a nightclub hostess Adrian also gave the nine-week treatment to. She stayed at his flat throughout the period, having sex with him twice a week. She paid him $1,500. Hoe Lai Ho, the elder sister of Kah Hong, was brought to Adrian some time in 1979 by her mother. Lai Ho stayed at the flat for a month of electric shock treatments and regular sex.

When Kah Hong was brought for treatment, Adrian prescribed a three-month stay. He said he liked her body. The day she came to stay at the flat, she was given the electric shock treatment. Kah Hong complained that it hurt, but he told her the pain was minor and he would have to give her this treatment once a week. He also told her about the sex god and its powers. "I invited her to light joss sticks and make a petition to the sex god. I also told her to swear obedience to me, which she did. Later I gave her and Mui Choo a glass of my urine and they drank it up." The next night, Mui Choo and Kah Hong were watching television when Adrian suddenly somersaulted, rolled and landed in front of his altar. He was only pretending, he said, to show Kah Hong that spirits could enter his body. "At the altar I went into a trance. I faked the voice of an old man and spoke in Malay. This voice was supposed to be that of the Old Master, Long Phor Luan. When they saw me in a trance, both of them rushed towards me. My wife was unaware that I was faking going into a trance. While I spoke in Malay, my wife translated into Hokkien so that Kah Hong would understand what I was saying." Adrian declared that Kah Hong was fated to be the wife of the Old Master and should consider Adrian the Old Master's representative. If she did what she was asked, all her troubles would disappear.

"Speaking in the same voice, I then asked for a ring. Mui Choo immediately went to one of my drawers and took out a gold ring. I put the ring on Kah Hong's finger and took a saffron cloth and bound her left hand to my right hand.

I then said that with the cloth, we both were husband and wife and Mui Choo was the witness. Kah Hong was amazed that I could go into a trance and did not object. I could fool her easily because she was the superstitious type and, furthermore, uneducated." Adrian instructed Mui Choo to trim Kah Hong's pubic hair as a sign of cleanliness as she was the bride of the Old Master. He took her into the room and they had sex. In the days that followed, Adrian taught Kah Hong to perform oral sex and to swallow his semen. "I told her that if she did as I said, she would be drinking holy juice as I was a holy man." He also showed her pornographic films and taught her to do for him what she saw in the films. "She was a fast learner and did as told. That is why I did not want to lose her."

Adrian said he killed Kah Hong's husband Ah Hua "because his presence was depriving me of having intercourse with his wife". After Ah Hua's death in January 1980, Adrian told Kah Hong to move out of the Toa Payoh flat and rent a room somewhere else in order to avoid suspicion. She left and stayed in Clementi, but visited often and they had sex every time she came to the flat.

The next upheaval in Adrian's life came with the Lucy Lau rape report at the end of 1980. Describing the frustration he felt after his arrest for rape, Adrian said: "I then slowly turned Mui Choo and Kah Hong to hate Lucy Lau and the police. I talked to them until they also became hostile and wanted to take revenge on Lucy Lau in any way they could. I told them that we could teach Lucy Lau a lesson by kidnapping

young children and killing them. In actual fact, I wanted
to kill young children and offer them to the goddess Kali
and then drink their blood. I wanted to do this so that I
could get Kali's assistance to get off the rape charge and other
troubles. Furthermore, I thought that if I killed children at
random and dumped their bodies, I could confuse the police
and make them investigate the murders and so, not look into
my rape case thoroughly."

Fear and folly

Mui Choo was 26 years old when she was arrested for the
murders of Agnes and Ghazali. In the seven years that she
had known Adrian, she had changed from a shy, lonely
bargirl to being a prostitute and stripper. She married
Adrian, but continued to entertain men for money while
witnessing a parade of young women, including her teenaged
sister, getting into bed with her husband. Several times she
helped to persuade young women to have sex with Adrian
and do his bidding. She was his partner in his work as a spirit
medium, acting as an interpreter when he was in a trance and
speaking in an unfamiliar voice or in Malay, participating in
the bell-ringing, chanting and other rituals at his altar. She
drank human blood before the altar at midnight and helped
to get the blood for Adrian's rituals. Mui Choo was also a
battered wife, beaten and humiliated by Adrian in front
of strangers and used as a guinea pig for his experiments
with electric shock devices. At his bidding, she had a long-
term sexual relationship with her teenaged brother, popped

tranquillisers, and had been arrested for helping Adrian when he raped Lucy Lau. She was also in the flat on the three occasions when death struck at Ah Hua, Agnes and Ghazali.

In her 31-page statement recorded three weeks after her arrest, Mui Choo said she only came to her senses at the CID and realised her folly. "When I first came to know my husband Adrian Lim, I believed that he was a medium and was able to read fortunes. I also believed that he was a Guru with many followers and had supernatural powers. After staying with him, I found out that Adrian was in fact a fake. He was not a medium or one who possessed supernatural powers. He in fact resorted to trickery to cheat people." She said that when Adrian set up his altar with statues and pictures of Hindu, Indonesian and Thai deities, he explained to her the powers of each deity. "He told me that the Indian deity Kali is in fact the Goddess of Mercy, and by worshipping her one would be able to get prosperity and pleasure. He added that Kali liked blood. Therefore, each time someone came for prayers or to drive away evil spirits, Adrian would ask them for their blood as an offering to Kali." If they agreed, Mui Choo would take them to a clinic at Whampoa Drive where the doctor would extract the blood and hand it to her in a small bottle for use later at the flat.

Adrian worshipped the Thai god Pragngan for sexual powers and potency, said Mui Choo. Whenever he desired a woman, he would go into a trance at his altar and say that Pragngan had entered him and wanted sex with her. "I would then play along with him and convince the victim that the spirit had entered my husband and had instructed him to have sexual intercourse with her. I did this as I strongly believed what he told me. Besides, I was also afraid of being beaten up by him. Whenever I disobeyed him, like when I failed to take my medicine when sick, drank alcohol when depressed, or showed signs of jealousy and temper when he had sexual intercourse with others in the house, he would fly into a rage and beat me up. He would also pretend to get into a trance and claim that Old Master had entered his body and then beat me up badly. Once he assaulted me until my face was swollen and as a result of that I am now hard of hearing."

Mui Choo said Adrian also made her recite verses to the deities before the altar, and on a couple of occasions she went into a trance. Later, when she could not get into a trance, Adrian told her it was because the spirit of her dead grandmother was following her and would follow her until the day she died. He told her she would be grumpy and would start thinking of evil things and would have sleepless nights because her grandmother's spirit would torture her. "This played on my mind and until today I have been tormented with the thought that my grandmother is in me and has been haunting me."

Mui Choo said that she began to feel a desire to die because it did not seem worthwhile to go on living with a spirit in her and following her. She became depressed and took to drinking alcohol and smoking excessively. She told Adrian that she wanted to see a psychiatrist, but he would not let her. Once Adrian told her that he wanted to die and she said she would die with him. He gave her 100 capsules and swallowed 100 capsules himself. She said she slept for three days whereas Adrian woke after a few hours. It was only after her arrest that she discovered that he sometimes removed the contents of the capsules.

Mui Choo said she dreaded Adrian's electric shock treatments. "The feeling would be terrible and I cannot describe it. My whole body would tremble. There would be a loud ringing and buzzing sound until I would either scream or become unconscious. On regaining consciousness, my head would feel lighter and I would feel better. However, there would be pain in my bones and my body and I would feel tired." Adrian gave her the electric shock treatment whenever he felt like it. "It was a nightmare receiving the treatment." Kah Hong's husband, Ah Hua, was also terrified of the treatment and became depressed and withdrawn after undergoing it. On the night he died, Ah Hua did not want to have the treatment and was frightened, but Adrian persuaded him that it would be all right. Of Ah Hua's death and the subsequent cover-up, Mui Choo said: "It was in fact Adrian who put forth his ideas and masterminded the whole thing while we followed like fools."

15 months with Adrian

Kah Hong was 24 years old when her mother took her to Adrian in late 1979. Fifteen months later, Kah Hong was arrested for the murders of Agnes and Ghazali. Her husband Ah Hua was dead, and she had lied to the police and a coroner about the circumstances of his death. In her 23-page statement recorded by Inspector Simon Suppiah, Kah Hong described her life with Adrian and Mui Choo: "I was brainwashed by both the husband and the wife. I was told that both my mother and my boyfriend had cast evil spirits on me and that my mother wanted nothing except money from me." Adrian and Mui Choo told her that a year after she settled down with Ah Hua, he would force her into prostitution. "On hearing this I became depressed and started crying. I spent sleepless nights in their house."

Every time Adrian wanted her to do his bidding, he would tell her that Old Master had entered his body and instructed him to pass the message to her. Kah Hong would then do as she was told. Kah Hong recalled a day Adrian told her to pretend that she was in a trance and possessed by the spirit of her dead father. She was to do this when Ah Hua and his father came to the flat, to persuade them to buy her a gold ring. It worked. Ah Hua and his father took her to a goldsmith's shop and bought the ring, but the older man said he would keep it until the couple's Chinese customary wedding. Although Kah Hong had been with Adrian and Mui Choo for only three months at the time of Ah Hua's death in January 1980, she said that by then she had been turned against her husband. Once she telephoned Ah Hua and demanded to know if he had cast an evil spell on her. "Ah Hua became sad on hearing all this," she said.

Kah Hong said she helped cover up the truth about Ah Hua's death after Adrian warned her that she would land in jail if the truth about his electrocution emerged. He briefed her to tell the police and the coroner that Ah Hua had been struck dead by a faulty fan. On the day of the inquest, he went over what she had to say once more. "Adrian told me that if I stuck to my story, Kali would give me a present and also take me to heaven when I die. He also gave me $100 for luck and told me that if anything went wrong during the inquest, he would commit suicide."

As for the Lucy Lau rape report, Kah Hong recalled that on the night Adrian was arrested, she asked Mui Choo if the beautician's allegation was true. Mui Choo told her it was untrue. After he was released on bail that day, Adrian came home and cried. "He began to complain that he had been placed in the lock-up and that he had been framed. He said he would be committing suicide. He told me he would leave all his property to me. On hearing this I too became depressed and told him I would go with him." Adrian telephoned her the next afternoon and told her that his Old Master had told him that his time was up. He told her to come to the flat after work. When she got there, Adrian gave her a chain with several amulets and told her to wear it. He and Mui Choo tried on their best clothes and told Kah Hong that those were the clothes they wished to be dressed in after they died.

Sometime after 10 p.m., Christina Chong arrived, having been summoned by Adrian. He now told Kah Hong that his Old Master had instructed that she should not follow Mui Choo and him in death that night. Adrian then took out a big sum of money and divided it between Kah Hong and Christina, telling them that they should not spend it until three months had passed. He then told Christina how to continue worshipping all the idols at his altar and what prayers to say at his and Mui Choo's funeral. Adrian and Mui Choo then dressed in their best clothes again and each swallowed a large quantity of capsules. Adrian woke up after a short while, but Mui Choo slept through the next day.

A day or two later, Adrian telephoned Kah Hong and asked her to come to the flat again. This time he told her that Lucy Lau had made a false report against him and he needed her help. He wanted her to go to the police and tell them that on the occasions that Lucy Lau alleged Adrian had raped her, Kah Hong was in the flat and no such thing had occurred. Adrian reminded Kah Hong that he had helped her to cover up the circumstances of Ah Hua's death and it was now her turn to help him. All along, Kah Hong said, she believed she had caused Ah Hua's death because Adrian told her that the evil spirit in her body had wrenched Ah Hua's heart, killing him. Kah Hong went to the police and lied.

On 24 January 1981, Adrian telephoned Kah Hong and told her to get him a "fish". She went out the same afternoon. Unsuccessful in Clementi and Queenstown, she went to Toa Payoh Central and the Church of the Risen Christ, where she found Agnes and took her to the flat. Adrian found the child suitable for sex. The girl was drugged with tranquillisers before Kah Hong carried her to the bedroom. She said: "Adrian went into the room and closed the door after him. Not long after, he came out and complained that his penis was unable to penetrate Agnes' vagina. He appeared disappointed and complained that he felt a pain at his penis." He then sodomised the child.

Adrian said that shortly after midnight, he pricked both of Agnes' forefingers with a needle. "I then sucked the blood from one finger and drank it. I then asked Catherine and Kah Hong to suck the blood from the other finger. They did as asked." Adrian smeared some blood on the picture of the Goddess Kali and lit some joss sticks. Although Mui Choo had said after her arrest that she suffocated Agnes, in her longer statement she agreed with the others that it was Kah Hong who pushed the child's head into a tub of water. Mui Choo said she held the child's legs while Adrian stepped on the back of Agnes' neck to keep her head immersed. When Agnes was motionless, Adrian brought out his electric shock device and placed live wires into the tub while Agnes' head was still underwater. He also placed the wires on the child's soles. 'I did this to make doubly sure that she was dead,' he said.

Mui Choo and Kah Hong said they carried the bag containing Agnes' body and left the flat with Adrian walking ahead of them. But he claimed that he carried the bag with Kah Hong. On the way towards Block 11, Adrian spotted a man looking out of a flat in one of the nearby blocks. Afraid that the man might see them, Adrian told Mui Choo and Kah Hong to wave in the direction of the car park to make it seem as if someone had just dropped them there. They then walked on to Block 11 and left the bag near a lift. They took a longer, different route back to their flat. Over the next few days, they bought all the English and Chinese newspapers to read about the discovery of the dead girl in a bag and the round-the-clock police investigations.

The day after Agnes was killed, Adrian told Kah Hong to get more children. "Adrian told me to get a male, so that he could pair them up. He wanted Agnes to have a partner," she said in her statement. Adrian hoped that Agnes' murder would keep the police busy, but he still had to report to the police station to have his bail extended for the Lucy Lau rape case. Mui Choo said: "Adrian then became annoyed and dissatisfied and decided to commit another murder. Sometime in the first week of February 1981, Adrian called Kah Hong and complained that the police had been harassing him and disturbing his sleep." That was the day he told Kah Hong to get another "fish". Ah Hong said: "He wanted a young boy. He then kept pestering me day and night and made calls to my place of work as well as at my rented room."

Kah Hong found Ghazali on the second day of the Chinese New Year and took him to the flat and, like Agnes, he was drugged. Later, while the boy slept, Adrian stuffed a handkerchief into his mouth to gag him and taped his eyes shut. When the boy began to struggle, Adrian took a length of gauze and tied his mouth. He carried Ghazali into the back room and was tying his legs with raffia when the boy struggled violently and vomited. Adrian said he then used the side of his hand and gave Ghazali a chop on his throat. The two women did likewise and the boy stopped struggling.

"I then took out a syringe with a hypodermic needle and drew some blood from his arm. I cannot remember which arm," said Adrian. He emptied the blood into a glass and drank it all. As he attempted to draw out more blood, he noticed blood oozing out of the first puncture. Mui Choo and Kah Hong licked the blood off Ghazali's arm and dipped their fingers into the glass to lick up the blood that remained. After this, they took Ghazali to the bathroom and drowned him. Adrian used his electrical device as he did with Agnes, to make doubly sure that Ghazali was dead. He placed the live wires in the tub while Ghazali's head was still in it, and then placed the wires on the boy's soles and body. Adrian, Mui Choo and Kah Hong then went out to dinner. When they got back, Mui Choo rested while Kah Hong massaged Adrian.

It was some time after midnight that the three of them dressed Ghazali and got ready to dump the body. Blood kept oozing from the dead boy's nose and although they stuffed cotton wool up his nostrils, the bleeding would not stop. All three said that Kah Hong and Adrian took the body out of the flat while Mui Choo stayed to clean up. While returning to the flat after dumping Ghazali's body, Adrian noticed some bloodstains on the corridor and realised that they may have left a trail of blood. Adrian, Mui Choo and Kah Hong cleaned some bloodstains near their flat and along a staircase leading to the lift on the fifth floor. Some people noticed the three of them crouching along the staircase and corridors, but each time anyone looked, Adrian shone his torch and asked loudly: "Where did you lose your ring, Kah Hong?"

Inspector Suppiah had begun his testimony by going through the first three statements from Adrian, Mui Choo and Kah Hong after their arrest on 7 February 1981. He told the court that he questioned Mui Choo and Kah Hong for an hour each and spoke to Adrian for one-and-a-half hours. They signed their statements and shortly before 4 p.m. that day, he charged them with murdering Agnes and Ghazali. Mr Knight went through the statements and the inspector pointed out how the three had differed in their accounts of why they killed the children, the details of the murders and how they disposed of the bodies.

Adrian blamed everything on Lucy Lau, the beautician who told police he had raped her. "The police therefore had inconvenienced the three of us, that is, my wife Tan Mui Choo, Hoe Kah Hong and myself. The three of us then decided to get even with the whole world. I felt that I had been framed and that the police had been blind. We wanted revenge and we had a meeting. We decided to kill small children."

Mui Choo claimed that sometime in 1978 or 1979, she began to feel "this emotional feeling of killing" and told Adrian and Kah Hong about her urge to kill. She said Kah Hong was prepared to go along with her and kill because she was fed up with life and volunteered to try and find the victims.

Kah Hong blamed her mother and family: "All my mother and the others wanted was money … The killing was done so that the person would not grow up to be an evil person like my mother and the others."

Each also differed in describing what happened after Kah Hong brought Agnes and Ghazali to the flat by taxi. Kah Hong said she gave the girl some chocolates, a drink and some sleeping tablets, and Mui Choo and Adrian gave the child an electronic calculator to play with. Agnes became drowsy and Kah Hong said she took the child into a bedroom and coaxed her to sleep before carrying her to the bed in Adrian's room. While Agnes slept, the three discussed how to get rid of her. At about 1 a.m. Agnes woke to go to the bathroom. Kah Hong said she took the child to the toilet and immediately afterwards, the three of them pushed the girl's head into a plastic pail of water and drowned her. The body was wiped and stuffed into a brown PVC bag, which the three of them left near a lift in Block 11.

Adrian claimed it was he who carried the drowsy child into the bedroom. "Kah Hong then came into the room and stripped Agnes. She played with Agnes' vagina and teased her for being like Lucy Lau," he said. The three had dinner and watched television and at about midnight, he said, they carried Agnes into the bathroom and drowned her. Adrian said he and Kah Hong left Agnes' body at Block 11.

Mui Choo's version differed significantly. She said the three adults played cards with Agnes until the girl got restless and wanted to go home. Mui Choo claimed that she coaxed

Agnes to sleep, singing lullabies. She described Agnes' death in these words: "At about midnight I took a pillow and suffocated her as she slept. When she struggled, Kah Hong assisted me by holding her hands and my husband held both legs." Mui Choo said all three of them placed Agnes' body in the bag and took it out of the flat. She and Kah Hong dragged the bag down the stairs and to the lift at the fifth floor and on to Block 11, where they left it. "On our return home we discussed the murder and I laughed it out with the others. We then returned to bed." She also said that she telephoned Agnes' mother some days later. "I asked her mother if she wanted any other members of her family to die and said one death is not enough. The mother just kept listening. I then burst into laughter and placed the receiver down. I then felt at ease and satisfied. I became cheerful after the call."

As for Ghazali, Kah Hong said he was fed tranquillisers and the three adults played cards with him until he became drowsy. Twice he was carried into a bedroom, but both times he came out and lay down in the living room. While he was asleep, the three went out for dinner. When they got back, they tied and gagged the boy, but he began to struggle and shout and the gag slipped off. "We panicked and decided to kill him before his shouts attracted the neighbours," she said. All three then carried Ghazali to the bathroom and drowned him in a pail of water. The boy vomited and defecated during the struggle so after he died, they removed his clothes and washed him. They then left for a seafood supper at Toa Payoh Town Garden. They took Ghazali's slippers with them and threw them in a drain. When they returned, they dressed the dead boy. Kah Hong said that at about 1 a.m., she carried the body and left it outside Block 10. Adrian's account was similar to Kah Hong's. He said he accompanied Kah Hong to dispose of the body.

Once again, Mui Choo's account was different. She said that when the three of them returned from their seafood meal, she and Kah Hong carried the sleeping boy to a bedroom and he woke up. "I immediately took a pillow and covered his face. I then pressed the pillow against the face. I kept on pressing until he died. While I was doing this, Kah Hong held the hands while my husband held the legs." Mui Choo said all three of them took the body out of the flat at about 1.30 a.m. and she was the one who carried the dead boy.

Inspector Suppiah told the court that as investigations proceeded in the days after the arrests, police returned to the Toa Payoh flat a number of times to take away various items. On 8 February, they took away a box of Cadbury chocolates, the book *Witches, Wraiths and Warlocks*, a plastic container with 74 tablets of different drugs, a pair of shorts and a bloodstained handkerchief belonging to Adrian, an electronic calculator, two tubes of KY petroleum jelly lubricant, two decks of playing cards – Ghazali's fingerprint was found on a nine of spades – bandage and gauze. From a shelf in the kitchen, police took a plastic container with 257 capsules of Roche 30 tablets. The police removed a bloodstained raincoat, a red plastic tub in the bathroom, a bloodstained blouse belonging to Kah Hong and found soaking in a tub, and a blue dress also belonging to her.

On 9 February, they took some hair from under the carpet and sofa, a syringe stuck in a bowl of ash below the altar, three syringes and needles and a plug connected to a short length of wire. He also took 13 containers of various tablets. The hair and Group B bloodstains matched Ghazali's.

On 11 February, Inspector Suppiah took Adrian to the flat and removed a box of skewers kept next to the altar. A locked drawer produced cash totalling almost $160,000, kept in neat bundles of different denominations. He also found jewellery, two books on occult practices, and two electrical plugs connected to lengths of wire stored in a box in the kitchen – the device used by Adrian for his electric shock treatments. He removed an orange plastic tub used in the electric shock treatments.

On 24 February, Inspector Suppiah opened Adrian's letterbox and found almost 1,800 capsules and tablets of sedatives and medicines for psychiatric patients. He took away more electrical wiring and a box of sewing needles used by Adrian for his egg trick. In Kah Hong's rented room in Clementi, he found 102 capsules of a tranquilliser. Experts who did a handwriting analysis found that Adrian's handwriting was the same as that on the notes found in the flat with Agnes and Ghazali's names and telephone numbers.

On 26 February, Adrian agreed to give $10,000 from the cash found in the flat to Mui Choo for her legal fees. Inspector Suppiah told the court he interviewed Christina

Chong Kim Hew, the Kuala Lumpur student who became Adrian's "holy wife" and she complained that Adrian had cheated her of large sums of money. Adrian agreed to return $50,000 and some jewellery to her. Another $70,000 was returned to her after the trial. Inspector Suppiah also went to two clinics in Whampoa and removed the medical records of Adrian, Mui Choo and Kah Hong.

Cross-examined by Adrian's lawyer Mr Howard Cashin, Inspector Suppiah said Adrian remained confident and betrayed no hint of fear throughout the period he was questioned at the CID. He was polite and related all that had happened as if he were dictating the events. He showed no sign of regret and even when told that he would be charged with murder, remained cool and calm. As investigations continued, Adrian was always cooperative, cheerful and confident. The inspector did not see Adrian praying while he was held at the CID.

Mr J. B. Jeyaretnam asked the inspector if there was any reason why he questioned Mui Choo first, after the three were brought to the CID. Inspector Suppiah said it was because she appeared fearful and he guessed that she would break first and cooperate.

He said Mui Choo answered questions in a mechanical, resigned fashion. "She appeared to know what was going on. She was just narrating whatever I asked her." Mui Choo indicated to him that she hated her past. "She claimed that she hated people because they condemned her and looked down on her," he said. But she showed no sign that she regretted being with Adrian. Inspector Suppiah said that on occasions when he chatted with Mui Choo and was not recording a statement, she told him how she had been beaten by Adrian, sometimes violently, and had undergone the electric shock treatment more than 100 times.

Mui Choo told Inspector Suppiah that at first, she received the electric shock treatment to cure her headaches and later, to drive away evil spirits. She believed she was possessed by evil spirits and told him that Adrian had said it was his duty to rid her of the evil. His exorcisms took the form of violent beatings and the electric shock treatment. Mui Choo said she longed to die and wanted to see a psychiatrist, but Adrian said there was no need for that. She told the inspector that she had sex regularly with her teenage brother at the flat. "She told me Adrian had told her that if she wanted to remain young and pretty perpetually, she had to have sex with a much younger boy and also perform oral masturbation and consume his sperm," he said.

CHAPTER 8

CHRISTINA CHONG: A "HOLY WIFE" WEEPS

Adrian Lim's needles-in-the-egg trick convinced teenager Christina Chong Kim Hew that he was a holy man with supernatural powers. Her life changed completely after a chance visit to his Toa Payoh flat in 1978. She became his "holy wife" and a prostitute, sending him thousands of dollars of her earnings. Adrian returned the money after his arrest.

Christina Chong Kim Hew told the Singapore police that she was 18 and attending a secretarial course in Kuala Lumpur when she came to Singapore. She moved in with Adrian Lim at his Toa Payoh flat, endured his electric shock treatments and beatings, became his "holy wife" and began having sex with him. At his urging, she began working as a prostitute and handed over more than $120,000 of her earnings to him. When he told her to return to Kuala Lumpur and continue working as a prostitute there, she obeyed him and continued sending money to him right up to the time of the child killings in 1981. She was working as a dance hostess at the Pertama Cabaret in Kuala Lumpur when Singapore police recorded a statement from her after Agnes Ng Siew Heok and Ghazali Marzuki were killed.

"I used to make regular telephone calls to Adrian from Kuala Lumpur. He would ask how much money I was making," she said in her statement. "I came to Singapore once a month to visit Adrian and give him all my earnings. On one occasion when I lost $1,700, Adrian assaulted me and told me that in future I was to send all my earnings to him through bank drafts. Adrian told me that his Old Master in Thailand died and he needed money for donations. Adrian used to telephone me and ask me for money for yearly prayers, Vesak celebrations and for prayers offered to other deities. Whenever I visited him he would give me a talisman, amulets and oils for which he charged me exorbitantly."

Sometime in 1979, Adrian started giving Christina his electric shock treatment, saying it would drive out the evil spirits in her. "He would make me lie on the floor clad only in my panty and brassiere. He would then ask me to grip metal objects such as knives, scissors and idols between my private parts and also in the strap of my brassiere. Then he would apply the current on my body. Adrian would also ask me to sit on a plastic stool with my feet submerged in a tub of water after which he would place two wires on my hands. The electric treatment was unbearable and at times I became unconscious."

She recalled an occasion when Adrian pricked her finger and smeared the blood onto the pictures and idols at his altar. He also pestered her to bring him virgins, saying he had a weak heart and having sex with virgins would make him stronger. He asked again when she came to Singapore at the end of January 1981, after Agnes Ng was killed. "Adrian instructed me to get him a virgin at all costs and when I told him that I was unable to do so, he became furious and scolded me. He said he needed a virgin to drive out the evil spirits in Mui Choo and me. When I remained adamant, Adrian told me that my business would dwindle."

Appearing at the trial of Adrian, Mui Choo and Kah Hong, Christina wept in the witness box on 7 April 1983 as Deputy Public Prosecutor Roy Neighbour read out her statement. Justice Sinnathuray gave her time to compose herself, before DPP Glenn Knight began questioning her. She told the court that she had resumed her secretarial studies in Kuala Lumpur. She said the last time she saw Adrian was on 31 January 1981, when he kept asking her to bring him a virgin for sex. Mr Knight asked if she ever took virgins to Adrian. She said she had refused to do so and when she told Adrian that the only friends she had were her former schoolmates in Malacca, he asked her to bring one of them.

Mr Knight: Did you in fact bring a virgin girl for him?

Justice Sinnathuray: Yes or no, when he asked you on January 31, 1981?

Christina: I just brought a girlfriend and I told her about this religion and everything and she was in the clear about it. So when I brought her down she was too smart for them and they did not manage to do anything to harm her.

Later in her testimony, Christina clarified that she took three girlfriends to Adrian, but they were all too clever to be tricked.

Cross-examined by Adrian's lawyer, Mr Howard Cashin, Christina described the first time she met Adrian and Mui Choo when she accompanied her friend Sunny Low to the Toa Payoh flat. "They were such a good actor and actress. They treated me so nice," she said. She went back by herself another day to have her fortune read. "I was curious and inquisitive about my future," she said.

When Mr Cashin asked why she agreed to stay at the flat after Adrian read her fortune, she replied that Adrian had gone into a trance, read her cards and given an accurate assessment of her character. He and Mui Choo were also so nice to her that she was won over. She stripped for Mui Choo to examine her body after Adrian said he wanted to drive out the evil spirits in her.

Asked if she felt she had to obey Adrian, Christina said: "I was more afraid of the Old Master that Adrian claimed he had in him when he was in a trance. Otherwise, I wouldn't have done it." That was also why she let Adrian apply his electric shock treatment on her. She was afraid of him only when he was in a trance because at those times he appeared fierce.

Mr Cashin then questioned her about the electric shock treatments. Christina said Adrian told her his Old Master asked him to give her the electric shocks and during the treatment either the Old Master or another god would enter his body and "drill away the evil spirits" in her. She underwent more than 50 electric shock treatments and Adrian appeared to be in a trance each time. "I just told him that if possible, I would rather not have the electric treatment but he said for my own good I had to go through with it, no matter how painful it was, to drive away the evil spirits." Adrian was cheerful and polite, except when he was in a trance. Then he would sometimes somersault and sit cross-legged in front of his altar looking serious, stern and even fierce. The crowded public gallery in the courtroom roared with laughter when Christina said Adrian held his cigarette in his left hand whenever he was in a trance, whereas he held it in his right hand when he was not. He also spoke in Malay and in a low voice when he was in a trance, but spoke English and Hokkien at other times.

Mr Cashin asked Christina about the day Adrian and Mui Choo attempted suicide, after summoning her and Kah Hong to the flat. She recalled them saying it was time to die and that they were fed up with the world. They rang a bell at the altar, lit joss sticks and wore all kinds of religious medals and idols on their bodies. They tied their hands to a leg of the altar table and swallowed 100 tranquilliser capsules each.

Adrian took a big bundle of money and gave her $100,000 and gave Kah Hong $23,000. He told Kah Hong that the money was for the funeral expenses for him and Mui Choo.

"He then wrote a letter, a kind of will, saying he would like to leave the flat to either me or Kah Hong," she said. Adrian told her the cash he gave her was for an overseas holiday so she could enjoy herself before following him and Mui Choo in death. Christina said she and Kah Hong watched over Adrian and Mui Choo after they swallowed the capsules and lay down before the altar. "They said they were going to leave for the next world soon," Adrian and Mui Choo fell asleep, but they did not die. "Adrian said that the greatness of the god or goddess decided that it was not time for them to die yet and that was why even though they consumed more than 100 capsules each they still didn't die," said Christina. Adrian took his money back.

Mui Choo's lawyer, Mr J.B. Jeyaretnam, asked Christina what made her think Adrian had supernatural powers. She said she was convinced by his needles-in-the-egg trick. She believed he had drawn the needles out of her body and after that, obeyed him when he asked her to stay at his flat and become his "holy wife".

When Mr Jeyaretnam asked why she endured the electric shock treatments, she replied: "Because they told me I was possessed by some evil spirit which was sent through my mother's side from Malacca and to wash away and clean my body of those evil spirits I had to go through this electric treatment." She said she found the treatment very painful and would groan or pass out during the sessions which lasted an hour or two. Afterwards, she would feel "very soft, very weak and very tired". Unlike her, she said, Mui Choo could bear the treatment for a longer duration, but the pain showed on her face and sometimes she made a choking sound as if she was "screaming softly".

Except for the electric shock treatments, Christina told the court she liked staying with Adrian and Mui Choo at their flat. Adrian was nice to both of them and even though he paid her more attention, Mui Choo never appeared upset. "She was very normal, she talked intelligently and joked. We used to joke a lot. Yes, we got along very well," she said. But Adrian also slapped her on several occasions. Just before each electric treatment began, he would slap her face and body more than 10 times saying he had to beat her because she was possessed. They were hard slaps, she said, adding: "I had no choice."

Mr Jeyaretnam: Did he suggest that you sleep with other men?

Christina: Do I have to answer that?

Justice Sinnathuray: Yes, you have to. When he wanted you to be a dance hostess, did he suggest that you go and sleep with other men?

Christina: Yes, he did.

Mr Jeyaretnam asked why she kept coming back to see Adrian. Christina said Adrian would telephone and ask her to come, and she obeyed and gave him her earnings to be cleansed of evil spirits. She gave him money because he told her he had a weak heart, Mui Choo could not work, and they needed money for medicines, day-to-day expenses and religious purposes. He told her she had no choice if she wanted her body to be cleansed of evil spirits and bad spells.

Mr Jeyaretnam asked if she could say to Adrian: "No, I am not coming." Christina did not answer. Justice Sinnathuray repeated the question, but Christina remained silent and just shook her head.

Christina was questioned next by Kah Hong's lawyer, Mr Nathan Isaac, who asked why she did not tell anyone about being assaulted and subjected to the electric shock treatment. At first, she said: "I just never thought of telling anybody, that's all." Then she added that she had been embarrassed to reveal this secret. "Well, I was worried that people might think that I am a fool for all that happened. [Yet], if I did not honestly believe, why would I keep on sending the money?"

Mr Isaac asked if she knew there were other women in Adrian's life besides Mui Choo and herself. Christina said she was not aware of his numerous other "holy wives" and it was only sometime in 1980 that she met Kah Hong. Even then, Adrian and Mui Choo told her that they pitied Kah Hong because her husband had died recently and she was mentally ill. Christina was not told that Kah Hong was also a "holy wife". She learnt about Lucy Lau as well, after Adrian telephoned her in January 1981 and complained that he had been framed for rape. He said he was having trouble with the police and needed $8,000 to pay a lawyer to handle the rape case and to make a donation to a Hindu temple to get the goddess Kali to stop the police harassing him. Christina said she believed that Adrian had been framed.

Mr Isaac asked her about the day Adrian and Mui Choo wanted to commit suicide and asked how she had reacted on being told that. She said she felt that if they wanted to commit suicide, it was up to them. But she knew that she did not want to die.

Mr Isaac: Why didn't you stop them?
Christina: Well, they are adults who can make up
   their own minds, not little kids. It is their wish.
   I respect their wish. That is all.

In re-examining Christina, Mr Knight asked how she would have reacted if she knew that Kah Hong was also one of Adrian's "holy wives". She said it would have made a big difference to her because she believed she was the only one. "Well, on the altar I rang the bell nine times and swore, right? That I was the only one chosen. So if I were to know [that there were other "holy wives"], I wouldn't have believed them any more."

Christina also gave the court an insight into Adrian and Mui Choo's lifestyle at their Toa Payoh flat. She said Adrian would wake up very late, have a meal and sit for a while before busying himself at his altar. He liked to listen to music, watch television and read the newspapers. They usually bought cooked food for their meals. "They ate well, and very good food too," she said. Adrian's altar work and prayers would take him late into the night and he usually had supper before going to bed.

Christina said she always found Adrian and Mui Choo quite normal. Only Kah Hong seemed reserved and, sometimes, sad too. The last time she saw the three of them at the flat was on 31 January 1981. It was then a week after Agnes Ng had been killed, but there was nothing unusual about them, she said.

Christina left the witness box after two days of testimony. Both days she covered her face as she left the Supreme Court building, determined not to let press photographers get her picture into the newspapers.

CHAPTER 9

DOCTORS SUPPLIED THOUSANDS OF PILLS

> Adrian Lim had an enormous stock of tranquillisers and other drugs which he dispensed to his "devotees" for a fee. Two doctors told the trial they supplied Adrian thousands of pills.

The next witness was Dr Yeo Peng Ngee, a doctor in private practice who prescribed tranquillisers to Adrian Lim and Tan Mui Choo and extracted blood from a number of girls Mui Choo brought to him. In his statement to the police, he said that he saw Adrian, Mui Choo and Hoe Kah Hong at his Whampoa Drive clinic. Adrian and Mui Choo complained most often of being unable to sleep and each time he would let them have 30 capsules of the tranquilliser Dalmadorm. Once, however, he gave Adrian 60 capsules.

Dr Yeo's records showed that over five years from May 1975 to September 1980, Mui Choo saw him on about 50 occasions and collected 30 capsules of the tranquilliser each time. She also brought several girls to the clinic asked him to draw blood from them. He did not keep records, but charged Mui Choo $2 each time he performed this service. He also supplied Adrian and Mui Choo about three dozen syringes. He sometimes let them have the syringes free of charge. "Adrian Lim told me they were meant for drawing out perfume essence from containers," he said.

Questioned by DPP Glenn Knight, Dr Yeo said that since November 1975 he had prescribed various sedatives for Adrian, who complained that he could not sleep, first because of marital problems and, later, because his nightclub work kept him up at night. Adrian brought Mui Choo to the clinic sometime in 1975 and introduced her as a friend. She, too, complained of having trouble sleeping and Dr Yeo prescribed sedatives. He said that he thought at first that Mui Choo's insomnia might be related to her being the other woman involved in Adrian's marital woes. He learnt later that she was Adrian's partner in his nightclub act. Dr Yeo said that over the years that he saw Adrian, Mui Choo and, later, Kah Hong, none of them had psychiatric complaints. Neither woman complained of being ill-treated, tortured or subjected to electric shocks by Adrian. Dr Yeo said that while he was a doctor in government service, he spent six months at Woodbridge Hospital and had dealt with psychiatric patients. He noticed no sign of psychiatric illness in Adrian, Mui Choo or Kah Hong.

Cross-examined by Adrian's lawyer, Mr Howard Cashin, Dr Yeo said that Adrian first came to his clinic on 4 December

1974 for a sexual matter – he wanted to increase his libido. Dr Yeo gave him a male hormone injection. In all, Dr Yeo saw Adrian four times in that month: on 4 December, he gave Adrian the hormone injection; on 9 December, when Adrian complained of pain at the injection site; on 12 December for diarrhoea and abdominal pain; and on 27 December when Adrian complained of feeling anxious. He did not think it strange that Adrian saw him four times that month or that those were signs of early anxiety neurosis. "All those years that Adrian Lim had been my patient he was friendly, pleasant, sometimes a little bit talkative," said Dr Yeo. For years Adrian saw the doctor two or three times a month, sometimes more. Adrian had 26 hormone injections in 1975, eight in 1976, three in 1977, one in 1978, and none after that.

In January 1975, Adrian complained that he had been "exposed to venereal disease". Dr Yeo admitted that he did not do a physical examination before prescribing Adrian medicines for venereal disease. Was it not a bit strange, Mr Cashin asked, that on the one hand, Adrian was asking for hormone injections to increase his libido but on the other hand, he was taking sleeping tablets? Dr Yeo replied that this had not occurred to him at the time. "I did try to exercise reasonable care," he said.

Justice Sinnathuray asked: "Was he the usual kind of patient that you had?" Dr Yeo replied: "It's not quite usual."

Mr Cashin pressed on, asking if Dr Yeo ought to have been more careful with a patient who kept coming to the clinic with all sorts of complaints and asking for all sorts of medicines. Dr Yeo replied: "I think I ought to have been more careful." Mr Cashin pointed out that over five visits in November and December 1975, Dr Yeo prescribed Adrian 150 Dalmadorm Roche 30 capsules. Dr Yeo admitted that he had over-prescribed, but maintained: "There are some patients who just can't sleep."

By the end of 1975, Dr Yeo had got to know Adrian quite well. He attended the birthday party of one of Adrian's children and even accompanied Adrian, his first wife and some of their friends to a nightclub. Dr Yeo told the court he did not want to go to the party but had been persuaded by Adrian's brother-in-law, a pharmaceutical salesman.

It was sometime in 1979 that Mui Choo started bringing women to the clinic for Dr Yeo to draw blood from them. Over a three-week period she brought about 10 young Malay women. The first time she showed up with two women, she told him Adrian needed the blood for prayers.

Dr Yeo told the court that he tried to say no, but Mui Choo was persistent. "She kept on saying, 'I am a regular patient; please do us a favour, it won't take too much of your time.' It seemed to me that they would not leave my consultation room. Finally I agreed," he said. He did not ask the two women for their consent before drawing their blood because they appeared to have come willingly. When Mr Cashin pressed him on this point, Dr Yeo replied: "At that time it did not occur to me that I should ask for their consent." He agreed with Mr Cashin that the situation was "completely bizarre and unusual".

Dr Yeo: It was a situation I could not handle. I did not know how to get them out of my room.

Mr Cashin: Doctor, you told us at the very beginning that the second accused said that Adrian wanted [the blood] for his prayers.

Dr Yeo: Yes, she did mention that.

Mr Cashin: I mean, surely that in itself would have been more than sufficient for you to say, "Get out of my clinic!"

Dr Yeo: That is what I tried to do, that is what I tried to do!

Mr Cashin: Are you not master in your own clinic?

Dr Yeo: Sometimes it was difficult, really very difficult, to get them out of my room.

Dr Yeo said he did not ask Mui Choo to tell him more about the prayers for which Adrian needed blood. Nor did he ask Adrian about it. "On looking back, I must admit I should have been more careful," he said. Over those three weeks that Mui Choo brought young women to his clinic, he gave in each time and drew blood from the women. "Each time I protested and finally I got very annoyed and very angry and that is how it stopped," he told the court. He said he felt very uneasy about drawing blood from the women, but told no one except his wife. Although he supplied Adrian with 30 to 40 syringes between 1976 and 1978, he never saw any connection between that and the blood withdrawals.

Mui Choo's lawyer Mr J.B. Jeyaretnam then took his

turn to question Dr Yeo. He wanted to know how he prescribed sedatives.

> **Mr Jeyaretnam**: If somebody comes and says, "Just last night I was unable to sleep, doctor", do you immediately prescribe Dalmadorm?
>
> **Dr Yeo**: Normally I prescribe valium.
>
> **Justice Sinnathuray**: If I walk into your clinic and say, "Last night I couldn't sleep", the next thing you do is give me valium? That is what you say, isn't it, doctor?
>
> **Dr Yeo**: Yes.

Mr Jeyaretnam then referred to Dr Yeo's police statement, in which he said Mui Choo was not suffering from any psychiatric ailment. Questioned by the lawyer, he agreed that prolonged sleeplessness was an abnormality and might suggest a psychiatric ailment. He agreed it had been wrong for him to say that Mui Choo was not suffering from any psychiatric ailment and that he was unable to say if she was depressed.

Cross-examined by Kah Hong's lawyer, Mr Nathan Isaac, Dr Yeo said he first saw Kah Hong in July 1980, when Mui Choo brought her to the clinic. Both women said they had venereal disease and he gave each an injection, though he did not examine either of them.

Mr Isaac asked why Dr Yeo never referred Mui Choo to a specialist when she had been complaining of insomnia for five years. Justice Sinnathuray took up the question as well, and Dr Yeo replied: "I should have, my Lord."

He saw Kah Hong on four occasions but did not examine or interview her to assess her psychiatric condition. He agreed with Mr Isaac that it was therefore wrong for him to have said in his police statement that he never saw any psychiatric ailment in Kah Hong.

The next witness was Dr Ang Yiau Hua, another doctor with his own clinic in Whampoa who saw Adrian, Mui Choo and Kah Hong between 1977 and 1980. Mui Choo was the first to consult him, in June 1977, when she complained of menstrual cramps and insomnia. He prescribed painkillers for her cramps but did not give her any tranquillisers. She came back twice in March 1978, complaining of headaches, giddiness and insomnia. On the last visit Dr Ang prescribed 60 capsules of Dalmadorm Roche 30. He said he treated Adrian only once, in June 1980, for a blocked nose. Kah Hong came to his clinic three times, in December 1979 and January 1980. The first two times he treated her for ear trouble and the last time for severe headaches.

Dr Ang said regular patients could buy medicine from his nurses with his consent and without having to see him first, and several times he gave permission for Adrian to buy Dalmadorm. Between 31 October 1978 and 1 July 1980, Adrian went to the clinic 11 times. He obtained 60 capsules on the first occasion and after that, took home 100 capsules each time. Questioned by Mr Knight, Dr Ang said he did not know that Adrian, Mui Choo and Kah Hong were seeing Dr Yeo Peng Ngee at the same time that they were his patients. He also said that Dalmadorm Roche 30 was one of many drugs often prescribed to patients with sleep problems and it had no severe or lethal side effects.

Cross-examined by Mr Cashin, Dr Ang said he first prescribed Dalmadorm to Adrian on 31 October 1978, after Adrian had told him that he was in show business and part of his act involved swallowing blades. Dr Ang prescribed 60 Dalmadorm capsules, some antibiotics and a painkiller. That should have lasted two months, but five weeks later, he gave Adrian another 100 capsules after Adrian told him that show business sometimes took him out of Singapore and the extra drugs were meant for his trips.

Mr Cashin pointed out that on 28 November 1979, Dr Ang gave Adrian 100 capsules of Dalmadorm. Just three weeks later, on 20 December, Adrian collected another 100 capsules of Dalmadorm, two boxes of contraceptives for women, and 100 each of Beserol, Sinutab and Norminon capsules for the common cold.

> **Mr Cashin**: Do you normally dish out hundreds
> of tablets?
> **Dr Ang**: No.
> **Mr Cashin**: Why were you doing it?
> **Dr Ang**: Because I was under the impression that he
> was a man on the move. He was moving about.
> **Mr Cashin**: Does it matter whether he was on the

move? You still armed him with hundreds of
tablets. Now one would suspect that you gave
him so much, he couldn't possibly move!

Justice Sinnathuray: November 20, December
30, January 9 … Three times, he gave Adrian
hundreds upon hundreds of pills.

Dr Ang: Adrian told me that he had to take more
pills to sleep properly.

Justice Sinnathuray: Is it advisable, doctor, is it a
good thing from his health point of view, to give
him these large amounts of pills?

Dr Ang: It is unusual.

Justice Sinnathuray: It is unusual. So wouldn't you
put yourself on guard in this case, since it was
unusual?

Dr Ang: I did not.

Mr Cashin pointed out that at least twice – on 17 March
1980 and 15 April 1980 – Adrian collected drugs from both
doctors on the same day. He took home 100 Dalmadorm
capsules from Dr Ang and 30 more from Dr Yeo each time.

Mr Jeyaretnam asked about Mui Choo's visits to Dr Ang's
clinic. The first time, she complained of menstrual pains
and then, quite out of the blue, told him she was taking
Dalmadorm because she had trouble sleeping. Dr Ang said
he did not ask her who prescribed the drug. He also said
he had no experience in treating the mentally ill and if he came
across any patient with psychiatric ailments, he would refer

them to a specialist. He agreed with Mr Jeyaretnam that it was unusual for a patient to suffer prolonged sleeplessness and that depression could cause sleeplessness. Dr Ang said that in December 1979 he treated Mui Choo for a perforated eardrum. Her ear trouble continued until the middle of 1980. During that time she also complained of giddiness, headaches and insomnia. When Mr Jeyaretnam asked why people get headaches, Dr Ang replied that sometimes it is because they cannot sleep at night or because they have injured their head or have a growth in their head. He said it was also possible that headaches can result if electric shocks are applied to the body.

Cross-examined by Mr Isaac, Dr Ang said that Kah Hong also had ear problems. Adrian and Mui Choo brought her to the clinic on 20 December 1979 and she complained of a ringing sound in her ears. "She said she worked in a factory. She told me that the ringing sound and a bit of deafness were due to excessive machine sounds," he said. A week later he treated her for a fungal infection in her ear and a lip ulcer. The following month she complained of earache, breathlessness and insomnia. He gave her painkillers, mild tranquillisers and sleeping pills.

Dr Ang was the last prosecution witness. After two weeks, the sensational trial had made the headlines in Singapore and regional newspapers and news magazines. On 7 April 1983, Mr Cashin reported to the Jurong police that he had received several death threats in connection with the murder trial.

There had been three phone calls to his home and one to his office, from men threatening to kill him. A woman who called his office said she represented a group of parents. To those who were unhappy that he was defending Adrian Lim, the senior lawyer explained that he had been assigned by the High Court to act as Adrian's lawyer. When there is a charge involving the death penalty and the accused either cannot afford a lawyer or does not engage one, a senior lawyer is assigned by the High Court to defend the accused.

Meanwhile, Canon Frank Lomax, Vicar of St Andrew's Anglican Cathedral, wrote to *The Straits Times* to protest at its reporting of the trial. He said: "I have read of your coverage of the Toa Payoh murder case and I feel compelled to write to you as one concerned with leading and counselling young people, to ask whether the detailed description of so much perversion and evil serves any useful purpose for the reading public, and particularly to express anxiety about its effect on children picking up the paper and reading those pages. I have always regarded *The Straits Times* as a very responsible newspaper, but I believe that questions need to be asked of this particular piece of reporting."

The Editor's reply, published below the priest's letter, said: "Thank you. Your point is taken – and, as you would have noticed, our coverage now reflects acceptance of views such as yours." The paper had started toning down its reporting of the case.

A week later, two more letters appeared in the newspaper's Forum Page, which at that time still published letters from writers using pseudonyms. A woman calling herself "Kiwi Mum" said: "I read with great interest Canon Frank Lomax's letter regarding the reporting of the Toa Payoh murder trial. I would like to endorse his views entirely. I was very surprised at the intense publicity given to the case. What is good reporting if discretion is not used to some extent when it ultimately concerns the trauma of the families involved? Since coming to live here, I have greatly appreciated the capacity of *The Straits Times* with its directness in reporting. Let more consideration be given, however, to the extensive age group that reads this media. Children, especially, are so easily influenced."

But reader James Lam had this to say: "Contrary to what some others might say, I think the coverage of the Toa Payoh murder trial is well done. In fact, it could very well serve as a warning to people, especially young gullible women, to be more alert and careful when they encounter a similar situation. It also serves as a reminder to parents to educate their children to be more wary of strangers. Perhaps the open trial itself serves to educate the general public to open its eyes to the fact that this sort of thing could happen and has happened in our society. If it was thought that details of the trial could in any way harm the morals of the public, then I am sure it would have been heard in camera from the beginning. Thanks for the good reporting."

Over at the Supreme Court, the Toa Payoh "ritual killings" trial continued. The next witness was Adrian, ensuring unabated interest in the case.

CHAPTER 10

ADRIAN IN THE WITNESS STAND: "I AM A LADIES' MAN"

> Over five days in the witness stand, Adrian
> Lim insisted he was the only one responsible
> for killing Agnes Ng Siew Heok and Ghazali
> Marzuki, and that Tan Mui Choo and Hoe
> Kah Hong should not be blamed. There were
> several questions about the supernatural that
> he refused to answer, saying: "No comment."

There was a hush in the crowded courtroom as a prison officer led Adrian Lim from the dock to the witness stand on 13 April 1983. Dressed in a white T-shirt and brown trousers and holding a Roman Catholic rosary in one hand, he was about to begin five days of testimony. He took his oath on the Bible and asked for his spectacles. When his lawyer, Mr. Howard Cashin, asked him to state his full name, Adrian turned to Justice T. S. Sinnathuray and Justice F. A. Chua and said: "My Lords, I am sorry, could I say something? I have something to say." Justice Sinnathuray told him to

state his name and advised him to answer the questions put
to him by counsel.

> **Adrian**: But my Lord, I wish to say something.
>
> **Mr Cashin**: OK, tell my Lord.
>
> **Adrian**: Thank you. My Lord, as we all know that
> there are no eyewitnesses…
>
> **Justice Sinnathuray**: No, no, we don't want a speech
> from him.
>
> **Adrian**: It's a confession, my Lord.
>
> **Justice Sinnathuray**: Mr Cashin will take you
> through it.

This early exchange between Adrian, his lawyer and the
judge was a foretaste of things to come. They were five long
days for Adrian, as he was questioned by his lawyer, the
judges, as well as Mr J.B. Jeyaretnam, representing Tan Mui
Choo, Mr Nathan Isaac, representing Hoe Kah Hong, and
Deputy Public Prosecutor Glenn Knight.

Adrian repeated several times on the first day that he
wished to be "honest and fair" in what he told the court.
Extremely respectful towards the judges, he frequently left the
lawyers exasperated by his refusal to answer questions, saying
he did not wish to offend the deities or the dead. His stock
response to such questions: "No comment." Often, he would
not answer a straightforward question with a straightforward
answer, and would seek permission to explain. Having got
the judges' consent, he would embark on a rambling reply. In

court, Adrian departed significantly from what he had said in his long statement to the police. He now claimed that he acted alone when he killed Agnes Ng Siew Heok, Ghazali Marzuki and Loh Ngak Hua. He insisted that Mui Choo and Kah Hong were not responsible.

Mr Cashin began his examination of Adrian by referring to his account of meeting Uncle Willie, the man who taught him the needles-in-the-egg trick. Adrian told the court that Uncle Willie was a medium, and at first they talked about spiritual matters. "You see, I am a Roman Catholic. I met this man, Uncle Willie, and he says so much about other religions, so I just get curious. So I want to learn, to study, research, to know more about it, that's all," he said. He believed that Uncle Willie possessed special, magical powers and he wanted to acquire those powers. He also believed that Uncle Willie could tell the future by reading cards and that he could prepare love charms and cast out evil spirits from those who were possessed. He had seen Uncle Willie in a trance, which he described in this way: "He looked like a monster. His face changed; he looked fierce, you know. He carried a knife in one hand and a rice bowl in the other, and his tongue would be sticking out. He spoke in a horrible way. It is not natural, you see, not his own natural self." Adrian then said that while he used to believe all this, he was now "puzzled". He recalled that while in a trance, Uncle Willie would poke himself with skewers and cut himself. "Uncle Willie would slash himself on his stomach," he recalled, laughing.

Mr Cashin: And what did he slash himself with?

Adrian: It sounds ridiculous.

Mr Cashin: I know it sounds ridiculous, but what did he do…

Adrian: That's why I was giggling.

Mr Cashin: I know, go on?

Adrian: With a big knife, a *parang*. Uncle Willie slashed his stomach, then his back, and this place and that place. There would be red lines where he struck himself, but only a little blood.

Uncle Willie had many devotees and Adrian said he was one of them. Uncle Willie taught him how to go into a trance. He added that when he had an altar in his Toa Payoh flat, "the trances were real". When he described how Uncle Willie taught him the needles-in-the-egg trick, Mr Cashin asked if that was nothing more than plain deception. Adrian replied: "It is a trick. As I said earlier, I want to be honest. I am honest. A trick is a trick."

Mr Cashin: What I am trying to get at is this, some of the things you learnt from Uncle Willie were plain tricks, tricks of the trade, trying to persuade people you had certain powers?

Adrian: Yes, that's correct.

Mr Cashin: And some of them were genuine, so far as going into trances were concerned?

Adrian: Not many. As I said earlier, it puzzles me.

Justice Sinnathuray: Was there anything that was really true that you learnt from him?

Adrian: I wouldn't use the word "true", but I would use the word "strange". Going into a trance, it puzzled me.

He admitted that the love potions concocted by Uncle Willie, using rose perfume, human hair and body fluids, were all fake. "I like to be honest," he added.

Mr Cashin: I want to know in so far as you are concerned, from your own account, you were clearly very successful in getting women yourself?

Adrian: I think it is my luck. I am a ladies' man. As I said, I like to be honest.

Mr Cashin then moved on to the Hindu goddess Kali. Adrian said he worshipped the goddess in only a few of her many forms, but when Mr Cashin asked him to name the relevant forms, he replied: "I am sorry, Mr Cashin, no comment … because I don't wish to involve goddess Kali or insult her." He said he believed in the goddess when he was living in his Toa Payoh flat, but now he was "puzzled".

Mr Cashin: Now Adrian, I am not trying to insult goddess Kali, but I have to find out. Can you tell me, did she require you to drink blood?

Adrian: It is a long story.

Mr Cashin: May we have it?

Adrian: You see, I am not the only one who drank blood. There were seven masters before me, they drank blood and I was taught by them to drink blood. You see, it started many, many years ago. It is not easy for a stranger to walk into a *bomoh*'s house — or you call it a witch's house — and say, 'Listen here, I am curious about your religion, I like to learn.' Now this man, when you walk into his house, he wants to get something out of you. He asks for money and, after money, there will be sacrifices and hardship for me and later, some testing, you know. And in the most final part, I have to bow to him and accept him as my guru.

Justice Sinnathuray: Who is this? Uncle Willie, is it?

Adrian: I am talking about seven of them.

Justice Sinnathuray: Seven of them?

Adrian: Yes, my Lord. So you see, after bowing and paying homage to them to humble myself, he will consider me his disciple. And after he has taken me as a disciple, we will go to a graveyard and there will be a ceremony and there will be other witnesses around, his disciples, and he will ask me to drink blood. That's why I said I didn't want to talk about it. Disgusting, you know.

Adrian said that there were seven men at the graveyard ceremony when his master handed him a cup of blood. "After I drank a big mouthful, I had to pass it back to my so-called master who drank and passed it to his disciples. So I am not the only one who drank blood."

Mr Cashin then questioned him about Kah Hong's husband, Ah Hua. Adrian said that Ah Hua and his father were mediums. Ah Hua had gone into a trance before the altar at the Toa Payoh flat and "he was havoc". Adrian was hesitant to elaborate, saying: "Well, you see, I respect the dead, that is, the deceased Loh Ngak Hua. I like to make it clear, Loh Ngak Hua, when he went into a trance, the deity or the saint or the god that possessed him was known as the First Prince of Heaven of the Taoist World. Loh Ngak Hua's father, when he was in a trance, claimed to be Guan Gong, the Taoist World's God of War."

Mr Cashin asked several times what he meant when he said that Ah Hua was "havoc" at the altar, but Adrian replied: "I'm sorry, Mr Cashin, I respect the dead. Let them rest in peace. I don't want to talk about it."

Justice Sinnathuray: But you must explain to us.

Adrian: I am sorry, my Lord.

Justice Sinnathuray: You said something. What is it that you mean by "havoc"?

Adrian: Something unpleasant.

Justice Sinnathuray: Of what kind?

Adrian: I cannot say, my Lord.

Mr Cashin: Did he insult Kali in one of her forms?

Adrian: No comment. I respect the dead. Let them rest in peace.

Mr Cashin: Were you angry with him?

Adrian: No comment.

Mr Cashin: By "no comment", do I take it that your answer is "Yes"?

Adrian: Take it as you like.

Mr Cashin then asked Adrian if, as a result of what had happened before the altar, he thought that Ah Hua should die. Adrian refused to say anything apart from confirming that Ah Hua had been electrocuted.

Justice Sinnathuray: Can you tell me briefly how he was electrocuted?

Adrian: I murdered him, my Lord.

Mr Cashin: Revenge for "havoc" at the altar?

Adrian: No comment.

When the judge asked him to confirm or deny the account in his police statement of Ah Hua's death, Adrian said once again that he had "no comment".

Exasperated, Justice Sinnathuray said: "No, no, no, Adrian Lim, you can't keep saying that to me." Turning to Mr Cashin, the judge said: "He is your witness."

Mr Cashin replied: "You can see now, my Lord, how difficult it is with this witness."

The lawyer continued questioning and coaxing Adrian, who eventually said: "Let me make it clear. As I have said, I murdered him. Now I will tell you how. Take the wire and electrocute him, that's all." Adrian said that he prayed before his altar and went into a trance before he electrocuted Ah Hua. When Mr Cashin asked whom Adrian had prayed to before Ah Hua's death, Adrian replied: "Many of them. Many deities, including Kali." Asked if the deities had told him what to do, Adrian replied: "No comment." He said he used his electric device on Ah Hua and Kah Hong, but applied more electricity to Ah Hua and that was how he died. "And I am responsible, my Lord," he added. He refused to answer when asked if the deities had instructed him to kill Ah Hua.

> **Adrian**: I am trying to say that murder has been committed. It is not fair for me to come into the witness box and start slandering all the religions – "I did it because Goddess Kali asked me to do it" – it is not fair, you see. And there is no proof that Goddess Kali asked me to do it … I am a sensible man … I enjoy your questioning. You can question me as much as you want.
>
> **Mr Cashin**: While in a trance, did you spiritually converse with the deities, talk to them, get answers from them?
>
> **Adrian**: All I can say is this, Mr Cashin … you are the best lawyer in town but I am so sorry. All

I can tell you is a little bit. I can't tell you too
much, a little bit, out of respect, you see.

Justice Sinnathuray: So what is your answer?

Adrian: My answer is, I had a strange and nice
feeling. Whether I talk to them, or they come
and meet me in my home when I am asleep –
no comment.

Mr Cashin moved on to asking about the large quantity
of drugs found in the Toa Payoh flat. Adrian said that in the
five years before his arrest, he consumed an assortment of
about 20 pills a day and they made him feel nice. Mui Choo
and Kah Hong took about 10 pills a day each. Adrian said he
got his supplies from the two doctors in Whampoa, as well as
two others in Toa Payoh and two of his brothers-in-law who
were pharmaceutical salesmen.

He said he devised his electric shock treatment after
learning that mentally ill patients were sometimes treated
with electricity. He tested the device on himself first. "At
first, it's a shock. Then you see travelling lights … it travels
in a very funny pattern," he said, running his fingers across
his forehead. "It's like a picture… Before you put it to your
head, you have to close your eyes and once you close your
eyes, you see light, like flashes." Adrian said he felt some pain
too, at the points where he applied his electrical device to his
head. He later used it on Mui Choo, Christina Chong, Kah
Hong, Kah Hong's mother and sister, as well as Ah Hua and
his father. He said he never forced Mui Choo to undergo

the electric shock treatment and, in fact, she liked it for her headaches and had the treatment five times a month on alternate months.

Mr Cashin then asked Adrian about his feelings for Mui Choo. He replied that he was fond of her, but believed she was possessed by evil spirits. "It's a long story," he said. Asked to tell it anyway, he said: "All I can say is this. Sometimes, late in the night, when I woke to get a drink of cold water, I saw her sleeping with her tongue sticking out. She looked like the goddess Kali … It was disgusting, my Lord." He said he took Mui Choo to several *bomoh*s to cure her of that habit and when all of them failed, he decided to treat her himself. At first he tried talking to her about the problem, but that did not work. Then they tried praying, by reciting the rosary before the picture of Jesus Christ left in the flat by his first wife. For a while after that, Mui Choo slept without sticking out her tongue. But the main problem, he said, was that she was possessed by the Third Prince of the Taoist World. He explained that this was a "very mischievous" spirit who created havoc whenever Mui Choo was taken to *bomoh*s. She would go into a trance and start abusing the *bomoh*s. This happened around 1978. Adrian recalled that many sleepless nights went by before he managed to get rid of the Third Prince. Mr Cashin informed the judges that this was the first time he had heard any of this.

Adrian was reluctant to talk about his show business past, saying: "If I keep on talking, a lot of people will get involved and the newspapers will have tons to write about and make tons of money and what do I get? So, we just talk about the murder … Past is past, I am not proud about it. I am a humble person." He did say, however, that he and Mui Choo performed together on and off between 1976 and 1980. He also said that he slapped Mui Choo occasionally, but not very hard. "I didn't enjoy slapping her."

Adrian told the court that he found himself surrounded by people who were possessed or were mediums — Mui Choo, Kah Hong and her mother, Ah Hua and his father. Kah Hong was possessed by the Goddess of Hell. "Only one spirit possessed her, but that one was dynamite. It was a terror." He took her to a Hindu holy man at a Serangoon Road temple several times but the man failed to drive out the Goddess of Hell. He allowed Kah Hong to stay at his flat because she was his "holy wife". Her bad temper persisted and she would be wild, aggressive and insulting when she flew into a rage. She would scream and shout, pick up drinking glasses and smash them. Adrian said he slapped her whenever she was in a rage. He tried praying before his altar with Kah Hong and that seemed to work and after worshipping several deities, she seemed to calm down and improve. But then she would return to her old ways.

Adrian then told the court about the day he sat before his altar with Mui Choo, who was possessed by the Third Prince, and Kah Hong, who was possessed by the Goddess of Hell. "I told Kah Hong that I had enough of this nonsense. I wanted peace, so stop giving me more headaches and havoc. But she said to me, 'It's not me.' I said, 'How come you acted strangely and differently?' She said, 'I am possessed, what can I do?' So I said, 'I'll try slapping you. Either you change or I'll try something else.' Then, before I could finish, both of them went into a trance and started mocking. They were havoc, violent and all sorts of things. Then she was saying something, not with her voice but with some strange voice. She said, 'It's the Goddess of Hell.' And the other one – Mui Choo – says, 'Ah, I am the Third Prince. We won't leave this body. You try and get rid of us.' So I said, 'Either you leave my wife alone or I'll give you hell. You're giving me hell, I'll return you to hell.' She said, 'Try.' So I went to the drawer, took out the electric wire and showed it to both of them. I said, 'Better behave yourselves.' But they were both in a violent trance and laughing away. One of them said, 'Maybe you can get rid of us temporarily but like the wind we came in, like the wind we'll go back.' So, in other words, there was no guarantee of getting rid of them. So I got annoyed and I said, 'Either you leave them or I'll give you electricity and see whether you are a real god.'"

Adrian said the spirits went away after he gave Mui Choo and Kah Hong the electric shock treatment, but they kept coming back. That was why he had to continue their electric shock treatments.

Adrian was more forthcoming when he was asked about Lucy Lau, the beautician who accused him of rape. He insisted on telling the court his version of events. He said that whenever Lucy came to the flat to discuss cosmetics and skin care with Mui Choo, he left them alone and his exchanges with Lucy were casual and brief. "But as time went by, I was just unlucky, she got attracted to me. So we became more friendly." He told her she should dress better, and she complained that her father took away most of her earnings. "So I said, 'If you have no objection to being my guest, I'll give you money.' And she said, 'OK.' Even on her birthday, I gave her. I was giving, giving, giving and she was friendly, friendly, friendly, closer, closer, closer."

Justice Sinnathuray: "Friendly, friendly, friendly; we got closer, closer, closer." Yes, go on, tell us.

Adrian: I mean, it's natural, my Lord.

Justice Sinnathuray: What?

Adrian: I mean, it is only natural, we became more friendly and closer, and that is how we did it.

Justice Sinnathuray: So you had sexual intercourse with her?

Adrian: Yes. It takes two to do it, not one.

Mr Cashin: Tell me, did you think that you had raped her?

Adrian: I beg your pardon? Rubbish!

He said he was furious when Lucy accused him of rape. "It's not easy to rape a girl, you know," he said. He complained that the police officers investigating the rape report mocked him and made fun of him and that made him angrier and more fed up. His wife, Mui Choo, was also arrested for helping him commit rape. His anger was beyond control, he said. He said he had sex with Lucy Lau on more than 30 occasions before she accused him of rape, just because he refused to bow to her wishes. "She is possessive. You cannot do this, you cannot do that. You can do this, you can do that, as though I was married to her for 10 years," he said. Adrian then told the court of a specific incident which, he was convinced, prompted Lucy to go to the police. He said he was having sex with Lucy at the flat one day, when Christina Chong telephoned from Kuala Lumpur. Lucy asked him afterwards who had called: "I said, 'One of my holy wives.' She said, 'You rascal!' I said, 'What do you mean, rascal? I have many holy wives.' She said, 'Why didn't you tell me?' I said, 'You never asked me, how can I tell you?'" Lucy insisted that he should break off with all his "holy wives". "I said, 'There are about 40 of them. You don't expect me to give up everything in a day?' " He said Lucy threatened to cause trouble for him if he did not drop his other "holy wives" immediately. "So I told her, 'I will not break my friendship with all my holy wives. She said, 'Either you do it or I will cause you trouble.' But what trouble, I did not know, until the police came. She is jealous."

Adrian said that after the rape report, he decided to do something, like murder, but he did not have anybody in mind. "I got fed up. I just got fed up," he said. He did not know Agnes and Ghazali, but he murdered them. It was his decision to murder the children, he said, adding that this was the confession he wanted to make at the start of his testimony.

Mr Cashin referred to Adrian's police statement, in which

he said he had asked Mui Choo and Kah Hong to bring him three children each. Adrian told the court that that was untrue. "I only wanted a pair … a boy and a girl." When Mr Cashin asked why he wanted a boy and a girl, he replied: "I told you I murdered them." Mr Cashin pressed on: "I know you have already told us that, but is there any particular reason why?" Adrian replied: "Spiritual sacrifice, my Lord."

When Mr Cashin asked if the decision to murder had anything to do with the rape report, Adrian replied: "No comment." Justice Sinnathuray told him: "You have just said that it was as a spiritual sacrifice that you murdered the children." Adrian said: "That is unfortunate."

When the judge asked again if the murders had anything to do with the rape report, Adrian replied: "I don't want to talk about it. I am getting groggy. We talk about murder, don't talk about Lucy – she gave me a lot of trouble." He became angry when Mr Cashin referred to the part of the police statement where he admitted having raped Lucy. Reading from the statement, Adrian said: "This part is wrong – 'I also confessed to Kah Hong that I had raped Lucy Lau' – it's rubbish. I mean, the rape is mentioned here and there and everywhere … Lucy Lau was my holy wife. I don't rape my own wife!"

Justice Sinnathuray: Lucy Lau was your "holy wife"?
Adrian: Yes. We got married at the altar. I even bought jewellery for her and then she goes around and yells rape. What a joke!

Adrian could not remember telling Inspector Richard Pereira, who recorded his statement, that he killed the two children as a form of revenge against Lucy. He now maintained that he killed the children as a spiritual sacrifice and denied that he had sex with either of them. "I had so many holy wives. Why should I want to do such a thing?"

He told the court that he killed Agnes himself. He said he smothered her with a pillow, drowned her in the bathroom and, to make sure she was dead, electrocuted her. He said he killed Ghazali in the same way. He insisted that Mui Choo and Kah Hong were not involved in killing Agnes or Ghazali.

When Mr Cashin asked him about his long statement and how it was recorded by Inspector Richard Pereira, Adrian said he gave "long answers to long questions and short answers to short questions". He said: "I want to be frank. Inspector Pereira, he is a gentleman. I like him. He has a way of questioning you. He smiles and says, 'Who is Uncle Willie?' I say, 'Uncle Willie is a homo.' 'Oh, is that so? Where is he staying?' 'Oh, he is staying in Changi.' 'Are you sure?' I say, 'Quite sure.' He says, 'What did Uncle Willie do?' Then I give him a long account and so on. Then, if he doesn't question me further, I will stop."

Adrian now claimed that not all the answers he gave Inspector Pereira were true. "I have to answer him, to oblige him. He is an inspector. Because if I don't, he will get annoyed, he will get angry. It is only natural, I don't blame him." He said he sometimes made up answers to keep the inspector happy. "I never thought whether it was true or not. I just answered to get it over with." He agreed, as the statement said, that he tricked many people with the needles-in-the-egg trick. He also agreed that he told Inspector Pereira that the powers of the sex god Pragngan were fake. "Inspector Pereira takes the statue and says, 'Look at it. Come, come. How can you believe in it?' And he says it's rubbish. So I say, 'I agree, it's rubbish.' Very simple, because what he says makes sense. 'Look at it; it's only a piece of wood!' I agreed, 'Yes.'"

The police statement he signed had a number of references to rape. Adrian disagreed vehemently when Mr Cashin referred to a part where he said that "all those with whom I had sex were actually raped by me".

> **Adrian**: You mean all those with whom I had sex were actually raped by me?
>
> **Justice Sinnathuray**: That's what you told Inspector Pereira?
>
> **Adrian**: Rubbish!
>
> **Justice Sinnathuray**: So that's rubbish?
>
> **Adrian**: You see, my Lord, I don't rape my own wife, you know.
>
> **Mr Cashin**: I was really thinking of people like Christina, Lucy and others?
>
> **Adrian**: Yeah, but they are my holy wives. I don't force them. I don't hold a gun at their heads?
>
> **Mr Cashin**: In other words, you don't agree now that you raped at all?

Adrian: There was no rape. That is what I'm getting at. It was all with mutual understanding, mutual consent. There was no rape … all rubbish! You can't rape your own wife!

Adrian's outbursts continued as more questions were put to him on this point. He said: "I don't rape girls – don't tell fairy tales! … Get to the point. You say I raped girls here. I am not a monster!"

Adrian was well into his second day in the witness stand when Mr Cashin ended his examination.

Mr J. B. Jeyaretnam then shifted the focus more closely to Adrian's relationship with Mui Choo. Adrian said that as a young man, he enjoyed going to nightclubs, parties and beach barbecues. He got to know many girls and had many sexual encounters. By 1974, when he met Mui Choo, he had already set up his fortune-telling practice at Alexandra Road. She had been brought to him by Anne, a Eurasian bargirl who told him that Mui Choo had family problems and needed companionship. Mr Jeyaretnam asked if Adrian could genuinely read fortunes from playing cards or if it was only a device. Adrian answered: "Just a device." He told some of the women who came to see him that they were possessed, but admitted now that he did not believe they were possessed.

Justice Sinnathuray: The end result was to have sex
with them?

Adrian: First they came to consult me and later on,
they kept on coming and coming and we got
friendlier and friendlier, we got closer and we
did it.

He agreed that he told his women clients to keep returning
for his perfume and ritual baths, but added: "They did not
have to come back if they didn't want to." Asked how many
women he tricked this way, he replied: "Many, many."

He said he took a particular interest in Mui Choo, because
Anne told him she needed companionship.

Mr Jeyaretnam: Anne told you this and you could
see it. Here was this girl who was 18, Catherine,
crying out for love and sympathy, isn't that so,
Adrian?

Adrian: Now let us be fair. Do you know that she
had an album full of snapshots of sailors with her
in a bikini? Let's be fair.

Mr Jeyaretnam: You mean even before she came to
see you she had photos with sailors?

Adrian: She was working in a bar crowded with
sailors and foreigners … she was fed up with
foreigners and sailors. They are brutal. Take a
look at the Champagne Bar one of these nights.
Loaded with sailors.

He said he wanted Mui Choo's body and wanted to stop her working at the bar. "I felt sorry for her, a good girl working in the wrong place." Mr Jeyaretnam then referred to what he described as a telling phrase in Adrian's police statement. Adrian had said that early in his relationship with Mui Choo, he "managed to get a hold on her". In court, however, Adrian denied that. "I became more friendly with her; she understands me, I understand her. So we became close and, as I said before, became friendly, close, and we did it. That's all." He brushed off Mr Jeyaretnam's suggestions that he gradually had Mui Choo in his clutches. "I don't agree," he said. "Ridiculous! How can I control a person? I am not God!" He admitted that he told Mui Choo about his supernatural powers and she believed him. He also lied to her when he told her he had a weak heart and needed sex with young girls to cure himself. Mui Choo believed whatever he told her, he said.

Adrian also denied asking Mui Choo to become a prostitute. "I didn't have to suggest it to her. She was doing it a long time ago," he said. Asked what he meant, he said: "She was having the sailor men. She had a talk with me and said, 'You don't mind if I go back to my old ways?'" Adrian admitted that he told Inspector Pereira that Mui Choo had agreed reluctantly to become a prostitute at his suggestion, but he now maintained that he only told the inspector that "to make myself look bad while she looks like an angel". He said he tried to dissuade Mui Choo from continuing as a prostitute but when she proved determined to carry on, he found her a pimp. When Mr Jeyaretnam put it to him that

Mui Choo was not only reluctant but also very unhappy to become a prostitute, Adrian scoffed: "Rubbish. It's a joke!" Mui Choo handed him all her earnings from prostitution, but he insisted that he only kept the money for her. He told Mr Jeyaretnam: "The way you are cross-examining me, you make me look like a monster. Do you know that after I married her she spent $25,000 on Joanne Drew [slimming treatments]? Ask her." He denied that he beat her because she did not please her clients. He said Mui Choo was a prostitute for about two years before he married her in 1977.

> **Justice Sinnathuray**: You married her despite
>   knowing that she was a prostitute?
> **Adrian**: Yes, I never run away.
> **Mr Jeyaretnam**: Well, I don't wish to be unkind to
>   you, but she was keeping you, wasn't she?
> **Adrian**: What a joke!

Adrian said that after her first two or three outings as a prostitute, Mui Choo contracted venereal disease. He took her to a doctor and looked after her for a month. He could not remember going into a trance and telling her to move in with him in Toa Payoh. Mr Jeyaretnam asked if it was true that he made Mui Choo swear obedience to him before his altar. Adrian retorted that it was not quite as simple as that. "We both agreed that we should love one another and become husband and wife. Then I told her, 'If that is your wish and it is also my wish, we should have a ceremony at the holy altar.'" So they went before the altar and swore their love for each other, with the idols as their witnesses, he said. He rang a bell nine times and from then on, they were "holy husband and wife".

Adrian denied that he asked Mui Choo to find young virgins for him to have sex with. "I had many already, so I never asked her to find any." She did ask him why he was always around young girls and he repeated his story about his heart ailment. "I had to tell her something. She was jealous, so I told her a fairy tale." He said he could not remember telling Mui Choo to have sex with her brother. He said the boy was about 13 years old when he came to the Toa Payoh flat and became interested in the various deities there, especially the sex god. The boy stayed at the flat for about a month and prayed to the sex god.

When Mr Jeyaretnam asked if he ever assaulted Mui Choo by kicking and punching her, Adrian said he only slapped her now and then. "I love her. Why should I kick her?" he asked. He maintained that he slapped her only for a good reason: to stop her drinking liquor, to stop her tongue sticking out at night, or because of the havoc caused by the Third Prince who possessed her. "I didn't slap her for nothing," he said.

Mr Jeyaretnam: My instructions are that Adrian slapped Mui Choo for all kinds of reasons – for not taking medicines, for not pleasing her male customers, when she was moody, for no rhyme or reason.

Adrian: The way you put it, it's as though I am insane, day and night slapping my wife for nothing. Is that what you are trying to say, that I am mad?

Adrian admitted, however, that he sometimes slapped Mui Choo while he was in a trance. He would snap out of his trance and find Mui Choo red-faced and crying, and she would tell him that he slapped her. He denied slapping her because she did not entertain her male clients well enough. "She is an expert," he said. He also denied slapping her for being moody. "She is a happy-go-lucky fellow. She is not the moody sort. But she's a good girl," he said.

He said he told Mui Choo that she was possessed because she acted strangely. She drank too much liquor and her tongue stuck out at night. "In our first year of marriage I asked her to make me a promise. I said, 'Darling, give up your drinking.' She told me, 'OK.' But each time she went shopping she would bring back Bacardi, champagne, Martell, all sorts of liquor. She pumped and pumped. Kept on drinking and drinking, switching on the amplifiers very loud and all that. So I got annoyed and I told her, 'Why? You want, we can go to a nightclub and drink and dance. Why do it in the house? You get drunk, you can't do your work, you misbehave.' It didn't work. I only gave her a few slaps, but it didn't work. Then one night I was going for a glass of water when I saw her tongue sticking out." After that, Adrian was convinced that Mui Choo was possessed. Mr Jeyaretnam said

Mui Choo had told him that there was no such incident, but Adrian replied: "In my opinion, it's true. She says it's not true but it is true."

Mui Choo had trouble sleeping at night and the problem gradually became worse, Adrian said. She also became irritable and moody, but he attributed that to her being possessed. He tried reasoning with her and slapping her but when that failed, he gave her the electric shock treatment and that cured her tongue problem, he said. He denied that Mui Choo screamed and passed out the first time she underwent the electric shock treatment. He also denied Mr Jeyaretnam's suggestion that Mui Choo dreaded the treatment. "We were very loving. If she lived in fear, she would have run away," he said. He denied that Mui Choo sometimes pleaded to be spared the electric shock treatment. In fact, he said, she would ask for the treatment after the nights when she could not sleep and sedatives did not work. "The next day she would tell me, 'travelling lights.'"

Mui Choo always prepared herself for the treatment by stripping to her underwear, placing the knives and other objects in the correct positions and sitting with her feet in a tub of water. After each treatment, she would take some pills before going to bed. For about a week or two after each treatment, she would not be irritable or moody and her tongue would not stick out at night. But after a fortnight, Adrian said, she would be "havoc" again. Asked if Mui Choo was submissive and obedient, Adrian replied: "Likewise with me. If she asked me to do anything, I would tell her yes. We both agreed with one another." Justice Sinnathuray asked if Mui Choo did everything he wanted her to do. Adrian said: "No, I couldn't stop her drinking."

Questioning Adrian about the drugs found in the flat, Mr Jeyaretnam noted that some were medicines prescribed to Kah Hong after she spent 45 days in Woodbridge Hospital. Adrian said Kah Hong was not a "mental case" but had been suffering from jealousy. She was treated for schizophrenia and after being discharged from hospital, brought her medicines to the Toa Payoh flat. Adrian said he tried all the medicines and they made him feel "sleepy, strange and nice". They also numbed the body. When Mui Choo saw him swallowing them, she had some too. Adrian agreed that Mui Choo wanted to see a psychiatrist but he felt she wanted to do so only because she was a copycat. They did not do anything about taking her to a psychiatrist because Kah Hong brought them a steady supply of psychiatric medicines. Adrian told Mui Choo there was no point in her seeing a psychiatrist as well, because she would be given the same medicines. Mui Choo was soon popping pills regularly.

Adrian said it was difficult to tell if Mui Choo was jealous when Christina Chong entered his life and shared his bed in the Toa Payoh flat for several months after becoming his "holy wife". He never noticed Mui Choo looking unhappy in Christina's presence, and if she was jealous, she did not tell him. He denied telling Christina to become a prostitute and he could not remember Mui Choo ever saying that she wanted to commit suicide.

Adrian maintained that it was his idea to kill children, not Mui Choo's. "I wanted to kill children, not her." It was also not the goddess Kali who wanted the children sacrificed to her, he said. Mr Jeyaretnam then referred to a sentence in Adrian's police statement where he said that Mui Choo and Kah Hong "believed that it was Kali who came into my body and commanded them to get the children". Adrian said that line was "too dramatic" and he had only said it to please Inspector Pereira who "wanted something dramatic". When Mr Jeyaretnam suggested that by the time of the child killings Adrian had Mui Choo completely in his power, he replied: "I have no power, please. I am just a simple human being."

Once again, Adrian insisted that he alone was responsible for killing Agnes and Ghazali, and neither Mui Choo nor Kah Hong was involved. When Mr Jeyaretnam asked why his courtroom account was so different from what he had said in his signed statement, Adrian replied: "I saved it to come to this court and tell the truth." He said that while he was awaiting trial he had been shown pictures of Agnes' corpse. "I said, 'My God, she died in such a horrible way.' It is only fair that I come here and tell the truth." He said he killed Agnes and disposed of the body himself. He could not remember all the details, "but murder has been committed, there is no doubt". Asked why both women had admitted taking part in killing Agnes and Ghazali, Adrian said it was because they had to say something during their interrogation or the police would have been annoyed. Questioned by Justice Sinnathuray, Adrian denied attempting sexual intercourse with Agnes or sodomising the child. He also said he did not molest her. He said that on the night that Agnes was in the flat, he had sex with Kah Hong who afterwards smeared his semen on Agnes' private parts and molested the child. The day Ghazali was brought to the flat, Adrian said, he gave the two women stern orders not to get involved. He killed the boy himself, he said.

The court heard more about trances and spirit mediums when Adrian was cross-examined by Mr Nathan Isaac, counsel for Kah Hong. Adrian said that when he told the court that Mui Choo and Kah Hong were possessed, he had not made up the names of the spirits himself. The women themselves, while in a trance, named the spirits in their bodies. Adrian said the first indication he had that Kah Hong was possessed was when she was lighting joss sticks before his altar one day. She suddenly flew into a rage and swiped at the idols, bell, glasses and candles arranged there. It was most unusual because she was usually the one who tidied the altar.

> **Adrian**: I asked her, "Who are you?" Then she spoke in a funny way, saying, "I come from Hell."
> **Justice Sinnathuray**: She told you that she was the Goddess of Hell?
> **Adrian**: No. I called her Kah Hong, but she laughed and said, "I am not the so-and-so you call. I am from Hell."
> **Justice Sinnathuray**: She told you she was from Hell?

Adrian: Yes, she was from Hell and her rank was
    Goddess. I told her, "You are from Hell, there are
    so many devils in Hell. Who the devil are you?"
    She burst out laughing – you know, a strange
    laugh, I would not like to demonstrate it, it was
    very eerie, and she said, "I am a high-ranking
    Goddess from Hell."

Adrian said that Kah Hong's mother was also a medium
and when she was in a trance, she claimed to be the daughter
of the Goddess of Mercy. Kah Hong's husband, Loh Ngak
Hua, had claimed while in a trance to be the First Prince of
Heaven from the Taoist world. A medium, Adrian explained,
was a person who went into a trance.

Mr Isaac: So, Adrian Lim, if I went to your house
    and stood before all your funny gods and I said,
    "I am the God of Heaven" and do something and
    pretend to be in a trance, you would say, "Isaac is
    a medium from Heaven." That is your definition?
Adrian: I would have said that you are mad, you are
    absolutely mad.

As the roar of laughter from the public gallery subsided,
Justice Sinnathuray urged Adrian to tell the court more
about trances. Adrian replied: "Take Mr Nathan Isaac just
now. When he told me he would go in front of all those
so-called funny gods and say, 'I am the God of Heaven', the

way he put it, I told him he would be mad. Because, it is he who is talking. I can distinguish his voice. He is only putting on an act. I can see him, his face is the same, smiling high and mighty, 'I am Nathan Isaac, the best lawyer in town.' " A person in a trance would speak with a different voice, his facial expression would change and he would be serious and unsmiling, Adrian said.

When Mr Isaac referred to Christina Chong's earlier testimony that Adrian held his cigarette with his left hand while in a trance, Adrian explained that there were two types of trance. A person who went into a violent trance would shake and tremble all over. Those who went into a smooth trance were always possessed by left-handed spirits and even though they may usually be right-handed, they would be left-handed once possessed.

Adrian said he did not go into a trance every time he prayed before his altar. But when there were "important things to be done", he would invite the gods to come. Sometimes they came and sometimes they did not. The various idols and deities at his altar were for his own meditation, he said, denying a suggestion by Mr Isaac that several religions were represented in order to attract people of all religions to have their fortunes told. Adrian said that whenever he was possessed, it was an ancient Indonesian deity, the Old Master, who entered his body. He had been introduced to the Old Master by one of his seven gurus, and the deity was represented on his altar by an Indonesian puppet. Adrian said he did not want to say more about the

Old Master as he now preferred reading the Bible.

Mr Isaac referred to one of Kah Hong's early visits to the Toa Payoh flat, during which Mui Choo wrestled with a python. Adrian said he bought the snake in Chinatown after Mui Choo entered a trance and the spirit which possessed her, the Third Prince, demanded a snake. So when Kah Hong, her mother and two sisters were in the flat, Mui Choo held the snake and pointed its head at them. Adrian denied having ordered Mui Choo to do this. He later slit the snake's throat, collected its blood in a bowl and made everyone have a sip. "I did not sip, I drank it. I was in a trance. Now if you ask me to drink blood, I will vomit. Now if I look at the blood, I will faint."

Kah Hong was friendly and came to visit the flat on her days off from work. She would get into a trance and behave aggressively. Adrian said he made her drink urine – his and hers – to get rid of the Goddess of Hell. He denied telling her that her husband, Ah Hua, was no good and would force her into prostitution after their customary marriage ceremony.

It was also untrue, he said, that Mui Choo took Kah Hong into a room, stripped her, examined her body and told him that Kah Hong had a good body with firm flesh. He said that when he eventually had sex with Kah Hong, it was by mutual consent. As for the incident when Kah Hong returned to her family home and smashed the altar there, Adrian said: "That was the Goddess of Hell, not me." He denied that he made Kah Hong swear obedience to him, or that he turned her against her mother.

When Mr Isaac suggested that he only wanted Kah Hong to stay at the flat so that she could be a servant and wash his and Mui Choo's clothes, Adrian countered: "Did you know that I did her washing too, and I washed her panties? You are getting personal. All of us helped one another." While Kah Hong was at his flat, he said, her mother and husband came looking for her. Adrian said: "I told her, 'Look, your mother is giving us hell, reporting to the police, coming here and all of you start fighting, and now your husband has come. That's the last straw. Why don't you just go home?' She said, 'No, I want to be near you.' So what can I say? I don't want to insult her, my Lord."

Adrian agreed with Mr Isaac that he planned Loh Ngak Hua's murder, carried it out and made it look like an accident to fool the police. Kah Hong knew that he murdered Ah Hua, he said, but she lied to the police of her own free will. He denied telling her that the police would blame her, or that Ah Hua had died after her evil spirit had jumped out of her body and killed him. Adrian said it was also not true that he told Kah Hong that goddess Kali would be happy and reward her if she lied to the police about Ah Hua's death, or that he threatened to commit suicide if she did not do as he told her. He denied that he confiscated Kah Hong's medicines after she was discharged from Woodbridge Hospital and told her to go back and ask for more by lying that she had lost her medicines. Adrian said he kept her medicines in the kitchen cabinet, but Kah Hong did not need the hospital medicines because she preferred Dalmadorm and helped herself to his supply. Kah Hong was not mad, but jealous of the other women in his life. When she found out about his "holy wife" Christina Chong, she flew into a rage, went into a trance and smashed the altar.

To more questions from Mr Isaac, Adrian said he could not remember any occasion when Kah Hong told him she wanted to commit suicide. Nor could he recall telling Kah Hong that he wanted to kill himself. He could not remember the mock double suicide attempt described in court earlier by Christina Chong. As for the Lucy Lau rape report, he said he did not force Kah Hong to lie to the police that she was in the flat on all the occasions that Lucy Lau alleged she had been raped. He denied telling Kah Hong that it was her turn to help him, since he had helped her to cover up Ah Hua's murder.

Adrian agreed that he asked Kah Hong to bring him children, but denied that he told her to go out at 6 p.m. because she would look like a ghost and it would be easy to lure the children to his flat. "I am sure that the children would run away from her if she looked like a ghost," he said.

When Mr Isaac asked again if Kah Hong ever threatened to commit suicide, Adrian said he now remembered her saying that if she did not have his affection and attention, she would kill herself. But he said he could not remember if she ever swallowed insecticide. He remembered also, that while Kah Hong was staying at her rented room in Clementi, she swallowed a quantity of pills and had to be taken to hospital. She had called him before consuming the pills and told him to give up all his "holy wives" or she would cause him trouble. She was jealous and they had previously argued about it. "She looked at the photo album and said, 'How come you are surrounded by girls? You have one there, you have one there, you have one there. I say, this one looks like a singer, this one looks like an air hostess, this one looks like a receptionist, that one looks like a waitress.' She grumbled and grumbled, you know, my Lord. You know how women are!"

Adrian denied Mr Isaac's suggestion that after Kah Hong's long stay in Woodbridge Hospital in 1980, he knew she was a mental patient and took advantage of the state she was in. He also denied telling Mui Choo that they could make use of Kah Hong and get rid of her if she proved troublesome.

The last to cross-examine Adrian was DPP Glenn Knight, who made it clear that he did not accept parts of Adrian's testimony.

> **Mr Knight**: My case is that you, with Mui Choo and Kah Hong, killed Ghazali and Agnes.
>
> **Adrian**: No.
>
> **Mr Knight**: When you killed them, you knew exactly what you were doing.
>
> **Adrian**: Correct.
>
> **Mr Knight**: I suggest that the reason why you are saying that Mui Choo and Kah Hong did not participate is that you want to help them.
>
> **Adrian**: I am sorry, my Lord, that is not correct.

Mr Knight: What is your defence on both these
   charges?
Adrian: I have no defence on both these charges.
   I am guilty, my Lord.

The DPP asked if Adrian was in the witness stand to
make his defence or make up stories. Adrian turned to the
judges and said: "There is no reason for Mr Glenn Knight
to cross-examine me." When Mr Knight asked why it had
been necessary to kill the two children, Adrian said only
that it was his plan. "Why, Adrian, why?" asked Mr Knight.
"Why didn't you kill yourself as a sacrifice?" Adrian did not
answer, and said once more that he had killed the children.
Mr Knight asked if he had no reason for killing the children.

Justice Sinnathuray: You didn't kill your wife, you
   didn't kill Kah Hong or yourself. Why did you
   kill the children?
Adrian: Because I needed them.
Mr Knight: Why children?
Adrian: Because I had in mind to offer children to
   the deities. It was my decision alone, nothing
   to do with the ladies.

Adrian agreed that there was no need for him to sexually
assault Agnes for the purpose of spiritual sacrifice, but insisted
that he did not sexually assault her. Mr Knight then asked
if he still stood by the account of the child killings he had

given the court. Adrian thought about it before saying there had been some errors in his testimony and he now wished to correct them.

He told the court that he was at his altar meditating when Kah Hong brought Agnes to the flat. He saw the girl, but continued praying. Then he lit incense at the altar and told the deities: "I will offer you children." When Agnes was asleep, Adrian said, he carried her into a room, placed her on the bed, lit incense at the altar of the sex god and had sex with Kah Hong beside the sleeping child. Afterwards, he left Kah Hong and went to wash himself. When he returned, he said, he was shocked to find Kah Hong stabbing Agnes' vagina and anus with her fingers. "I got into a rage. I gave her a slap and told her not to dirty herself like that. Little Agnes was naked on the bed." He then tied the child's hands and legs before smothering her with a pillow. The two women did not help. He used a syringe to draw some blood from Agnes and emptied the syringe into three glasses at the altar. He then carried the child to the bathroom, drowned her and applied the electric shock treatment to make sure she was dead. He and the women went out for dinner and late that night, he disposed of the body.

Mr Knight said: "You say that Mui Choo and Kah Hong never helped you in any way. Are you sure about that?" Adrian held out his left hand, showing the rosary coiled around his fingers, and replied: "I am holding a rosary! I have no reason to tell lies. I am a Catholic. I am not trying to get them off the hook!"

Mr Knight persisted with questions about the women's involvement, and Adrian agreed that Kah Hong had helped by obeying his instructions to bring children to the flat. But he insisted that she did not know the children were going to be killed. It was also his idea, he said, to drug the children once they were in the flat, so that they would not struggle when he drew their blood or smothered them. Mr Knight asked Adrian why he did not look for the children himself, if he did not want the women to be involved. "I didn't think of it," he replied. Adrian denied that he killed the children in order to confuse or distract the police from their investigations into the Lucy Lau rape report. He said it was a sheer coincidence that Ghazali was killed on the day that he had to report to the Toa Payoh police station to extend his bail, and that Agnes was killed the day after he had his bail extended.

Mr Knight then referred to Adrian's police statement, in which he said that he killed to take revenge for being framed by Lucy Lau and that he, Mui Choo and Kah Hong took part in the killings. There was no mention of spiritual killings, Mr Knight pointed out.

Adrian replied that he did not tell the police about the spiritual aspect of the killings because they never asked about it. Anyway, he added, he had saved that for his courtroom confession. He had only mentioned it to Dr Chee Kuan Tsee, one of the psychiatrists he saw while in custody. Adrian said this was not a "deliberate, black lie", but only an "innocent lie". Adrian said he was angry about the rape report because it was a ridiculous allegation. When the police started investigating Lucy Lau's allegation, he was angry with everyone and that was why he told Inspector Pereira that he killed the children to take revenge for being framed. The statement recorded by Inspector Pereira was "half true, half not true", and he told the inspector some "fairy tales", although they were only innocent lies. The bits about goddess Kali, for example, were for dramatic effect. Adrian said he noticed that Inspector Pereira got fed up if he gave short answers. "So, to make him happy, since he liked long and fanciful answers, I gave them to him!"

Mr Knight said if it was true that Adrian had killed the children and disposed of the bodies himself, why had the police not found any bloodstained shirt belonging to him? Adrian appeared surprised and said: "It's not possible. I was carrying Ghazali, the blood must have dripped on my shirt." He said he must have either thrown his bloodstained shirt or burnt it. He said he worked with Mui Choo and Kah Hong as a team in everything but murder. In the abduction of the children, each had specific roles: to play with the children to win their confidence, drug them and record their particulars. Justice Sinnathuray asked why it was necessary for Mui Choo to record each child's name, address and other particulars. Adrian replied: "Because, my Lord, you don't just kill a person and forget it. I like to know who they are, where they are staying … what happens if I kill my neighbour?"

He agreed with Mr Knight that Mui Choo acted as his assistant when he went into a trance and translated whatever he said for his clients. She and Kah Hong also helped to cover up the truth about Ah Hua's death. He agreed that he told Kah Hong to cry when Ah Hua's family came to the flat after Ah Hua had died. He agreed that Kah Hong helped him by giving a statement to the police after he was charged with rape, though that was not a lie because there had been no rape. He denied Mr Knight's suggestion that he was the type of person who would lie if he felt it necessary to do so. Mr Knight then asked a series of questions to show that Adrian would lie if he felt he had to.

Adrian denied that he lied to the police over the Lucy Lau rape case. Mr Knight pointed out that Adrian had told the police he never had sex with Lucy Lau, whereas he now admitted that he had sex with her more than 30 times. Adrian agreed that he lied over the circumstances of Ah Hua's death. He had lied to Inspector Pereira that the bloodstains in the flat were candle wax, and that Ghazali had come to the flat for help because he had a nosebleed. He lied when he told psychiatrist R. Nagulendran that he killed to take revenge over the rape report. Adrian agreed that he had lied to his first wife when she demanded to know if he was having an affair with Mui Choo. And he agreed that on the day his first wife attempted suicide, he had been prepared to lie by swearing before a picture of Jesus Christ that he was not having an affair with Mui Choo.

> **Justice Chua:** What the DPP is saying is that you are prepared to lie and swear in front of the altar of Jesus.

Mr Knight: You have no respect for the oath.

Adrian: You mean here? You are wrong, Mr Knight. Here I am talking about three murders, not about holy wives or enjoyment. I am serious. Innocent lives – three young, innocent lives – have been lost. I cannot afford to tell lies.

Mr Knight: My case is that you would lie if you thought it necessary.

Adrian: That is not necessary. I am sorry, Mr Knight, I wish I can help you. I am sorry.

Mr Knight put the prosecution case to Adrian once more. He said Adrian, Mui Choo and Kah Hong deliberately killed Agnes and Ghazali, and before the killings the three of them had discussed the murders. And all three took part in disposing of the bodies. Adrian denied it, saying: "It was I, not them." He denied again that he was lying in court to protect the women. "They don't need my help," he said. "I am responsible. It is not right for me to pin it on them because it was my decision." He denied Mr Knight's suggestion that he had played to the gallery throughout his five days in the witness stand in order to give the impression that he was a hero. "That's not correct," he said. "There's nothing heroic in killing children."

Mr Knight: In trying to help the second and third accused, you are trying to be a hero.

Adrian: That's not correct. I was never a hero.

Mr Knight: And you did sexually assault Agnes, didn't you?

Adrian: I did not.

Mr Knight: You are afraid of admitting that as well, aren't you, because you are afraid that the public might get the impression that you are not what you made yourself to be?

Adrian: I didn't make myself out to be anything. I came here to talk about murder.

Mr Knight: You see, a ladies' man would not go around sexually assaulting a child.

Adrian: You can say whatever you like.

He denied concocting the story of spiritual sacrifice for the trial. "What do I gain from it? No, I am talking about murder, not making up stories."

Re-examining Adrian, Mr Cashin noted that Adrian had said that he told various things to Inspector Pereira to make him happy. He had said that his police statement was "half true, half not true" and he had just told Mr Knight that his statement was "more or less" true. Which was it, asked Mr Cashin, reminding Adrian that this was his only opportunity to say anything he wanted. Adrian said: "Some parts are true, some parts, not true, and some parts, exaggerated."

He now said he had the idea to kill children as a form of spiritual sacrifice about a year before Lucy Lau's rape report. He said he had been receiving favours from goddess

Kali for several years, and in his prayers and meditation he had continued asking her to look after him. It was not the goddess who wanted human sacrifice, but he had got the idea himself. He could not remember if, after Agnes' death, he prayed and told the goddess that the child was a sacrifice to her in return for the favours he had received. Asked why he had given two versions of the killings – telling the police that he and the two women killed the children, but telling the court that he acted alone – Adrian replied: "I waited to come to this High Court to speak the whole truth." When Mr Cashin asked if all the trances he had described were mere pretence, Adrian replied: "I am puzzled. Because if you say it's a fake, it didn't look like a fake. If you say it's genuine, then I have no explanation. So the only thing to say, to be fair, I just say that I am puzzled."

After Adrian stepped down, Mr Cashin called two prison doctors as witnesses. Dr Naranjan Singh, head of the Prisons Medical Unit, told the court that on 23 March 1981, while Adrian was undergoing observation at the Changi Prison Hospital, there was a sudden sound of crashing glass in his cell. The fluorescent light tube was broken and Adrian claimed that he had swallowed some glass fragments. However, there was nothing to suggest that he had swallowed broken glass. The hospital's senior registrar, Dr S. R. Sayampanathan, told the court that Adrian hoarded painkillers and laxatives while he was held at the Queenstown prison later that year. Dr Sayampanathan said headaches and constipation were common complaints among prisoners and it was also common that prisoners went to see the doctor because it provided an opportunity to leave their cells. Still, the doctor said, Adrian saw him more than other prisoners.

Mr Cashin also called Adrian's younger sister and an aunt to testify. The court ruled that neither of their names was to be used by the Press.

Adrian's sister, a housewife, said that Adrian lived at the family home in Serangoon Gardens until his first marriage in 1967. "He was a normal person, he was a good boy," she said. "I saw nothing unusual in him." But he was hot-tempered just like their father. The family did not see much of Adrian after his marriage. He came to the house once a year at Chinese New Year but apart from that, mixed more with his wife's family. She said her parents visited Adrian quite often and told her that he was a very loving husband, a good father and a regular churchgoer. Their father, who had high blood pressure, died suddenly in 1978. The last time she saw Adrian was at their father's funeral. There was an incident in the funeral parlour when Adrian suddenly lost his temper and scolded their uncles and aunts, telling them that when his father turned to them for help, none of them helped him. Everyone was upset by this, she said. Cross-examined by Mr Knight, she said it was correct to say that she virtually lost contact with Adrian after his first marriage.

The aunt was a retired nurse and the younger sister of Adrian's father. She said that before Adrian's first marriage, he was always respectful towards her, and was a happy, friendly and talkative person. She did not see much of him after his first marriage. The last time she saw him was at his father's wake and she, too, remembered the funeral parlour incident. "Oh, he was definitely rude," she said. His mother wanted to stop him from abusing his uncles and aunts, but she was restrained by those around her. Adrian had come to the wake wearing ordinary clothes, and when he took off his shirt, everyone noticed the gold chains around his neck. "As Chinese, we don't put on gold to attend a funeral, so we thought that was a bit disrespectful to his father. But, you see, we couldn't do anything," she said. She did not see Adrian again after that. "His mother did not want to have anything to do with him," she said.

CHAPTER 11

TAN MUI CHOO: "I LIVED IN FEAR OF ADRIAN"

She was upset and jealous of the numerous other women in her husband's life, but Catherine Tan Mui Choo told the court she was too afraid of Adrian Lim's beatings and electric shock treatment to do anything about it. She said she believed all along that he had supernatural powers, and it was only after her arrest that she realised he was a fake.

Catherine Tan Mui Choo spent seven years with Adrian Lim. She was 19 when they met, and 26 when she was arrested and charged with killing three people – child victims Agnes Ng Siew Heok and Ghazali Marzuki, and Hoe Kah Hong's husband, Benson Loh Ngak Hua. She had also been charged with helping Adrian commit rape. She had gone from teenaged bargirl to accused murderess. Along the way, she became Adrian's "holy wife", a prostitute and stripper. She moved into his home while his first wife and children were still living there and, after his divorce, married Adrian. But there was no happy ever after, because he beat her regularly and subjected her to painful electric shock treatments. She assisted at Adrian's altar rituals and stood by as he made numerous women his "holy wives" and had sex with them all.

Looking back at her years with Adrian, Mui Choo said in the witness stand: "I was very disgusted with my way of life, it made me so tired and miserable. I was not happy." By the time she took part in the child killings in early 1981, she was completely under Adrian's influence. "At the time I had no feelings of my own. Whatever Adrian said, I just did it." She never disobeyed him because he beat her regularly, and she did not dare leave him because she was afraid of his supernatural powers. "He told me that even if I died without his permission, he would find my soul and I would not rest in peace. That frightened me, I dared not run away," she said, in answer to questions posed by her lawyer, Mr J.B. Jeyaretnam.

Mui Choo said she was unhappy and jealous about the other women in Adrian's life, but she had to let him do as he wished or he would beat her. From the first time he beat her in 1975, she began having difficulty sleeping at night. Later she suffered from insomnia and splitting headaches, which Adrian explained were caused by evil spirits possessing her. Adrian had told the court that Mui Choo slept with her tongue sticking out, but she denied that had happened. She recalled instead that Adrian told her she was possessed by many evil spirits because she attracted evil spirits easily. "I couldn't take it," she told the court. "I felt like I was cracking up." Adrian treated her sleep problem by dripping freshly-squeezed lime juice into her eyes. When her eyes smarted and hurt, he told her that this treatment would "blind the evil spirits". He also pumped lime juice up her nose. Then he devised his electric shock treatment and told her it would get rid of her evil spirits. "I agreed because my mind was so tormented by evil spirits," Mui Choo said.

The first time Adrian applied his electrical shock device to her body, it left scars on her head, thighs and feet. Mui Choo said she found it frightening and painful, and she told Adrian that she did not want any more, but he told her it would do her good. In all, she underwent more than 100 electric shock treatments. "Mentally, I became more stupid, I felt I could not think. I could not reason things out and when Adrian told me something, I could understand what he told me but when I tried to reason it out by myself, I could not. That was when I told him that something was very wrong with me and I needed to see a psychiatrist," she said. But instead of taking her to a psychiatrist, Adrian pumped urine into her eyes and up her nose. "It was torturing," she said.

Mui Choo admitted that she helped Adrian to administer the fatal electric shock treatment to Kah Hong's husband, Ah Hua, but added: "I thought these treatments were for driving away evil spirits. I did not know they could kill a person." She said she was the one who suggested giving Ah Hua the electric shock treatment because she believed he had an evil spirit in him after she caught him staring at her "with a kind of evil in his eyes".

After Ah Hua's death, Kah Hong was warded at Woodbridge Hospital. When she returned to the flat, Adrian took away her psychiatric medicines and told Mui Choo to help herself to the "mental pills". Mui Choo said she took two pills a day and Adrian gave them to Kah Hong on the days she underwent the electric shock treatment. Mui Choo said the "mental pills" helped her to sleep at night but also made her feel weak during the day. She was less irritable, but also unable to think for herself. "I was only existing at that time," she said. She agreed with Justice Sinnathuray that she found herself functioning like a robot. She also began seeing visions after Ah Hua's death. "In the middle of the night, when I could not sleep, I saw shadows, like a pumpkin, like Humpty Dumpty, with hands and legs, waving at me, calling me to come. Sometimes I heard the sound of temple gongs ringing in my ears," she said. After she started taking Kah Hong's medicines, she began gaining weight, so she signed up for slimming treatments at the Joanne Drew salon.

Mui Choo said she began to think of suicide, but she felt she needed Adrian's permission to die in peace. "I would tell him, if he did not want me, please let me go. I would drown myself in the sea and nobody would know. I wouldn't cause him any trouble at all. But he wouldn't release me. He always said nothing was wrong with me, it was only the evil spirits controlling me," she said.

Then Lucy Lau filed her rape report at the end of 1980. Mui Choo told the court she had helped persuade the beautician to have sex with Adrian. On his instructions, she stripped Lucy and examined her body. Adrian was very angry over the rape report and said he wanted to die. Mui Choo said she was anxious to die with him and their suicide attempt happened exactly as Christina Chong had told the court.

She said Adrian was at his altar one day in January 1981, when he went into a trance and said: "Time's up. Goddess Kali wants children." Mui Choo said she and Kah Hong were with him at the time. Adrian was still in the trance when he told Kah Hong that she would have to bring him children. When he snapped out of the trance, the three of them discussed what he had said and he said both women should try to get the children, whom he wanted to kill. Mui Choo said he gave two reasons for wanting to kill children: The goddess Kali wanted children, and he wanted revenge against the police for charging him wrongly with rape. "I could not protest," said Mui Choo. "At that time I had no feelings of my own. I could not think, so whatever he said, I just did it." Adrian said Kah Hong should get children first and Mui Choo later, but Mui Choo said she never went looking for children.

Mr Jeyaretnam asked how Agnes and Ghazali had died, and Mui Choo said Adrian's courtroom account – that he alone was responsible – was not true. She said that she and Kah Hong were involved in both killings. Mui Choo herself had given the police two accounts of the killings. She told the court now that it was not true that she once felt an emotional feeling to kill or that she and Kah Hong discussed killing together. It was also untrue that she suffocated Agnes and Ghazali. She said she lied to the police because she wanted to die.

> **Justice Sinnathuray**: Why did you want to take on the responsibility yourself?
>
> **Mui Choo**: When I found out at the CID that he was a fake, that he deceived me and all, I found it was no use living. I mean, he went to the extent of killing and all that, getting me involved.

She said that her second and longer police statement, describing how she, Adrian and Kah Hong killed the children and disposed of their bodies, was the true version of what had happened. On both occasions, she said, she was conscious of what she was doing and she knew that she was helping to kill a child. "I did not know it was wrong because I could not think that I was doing anything wrong at the time," she said. She was not worried that the police might be on their trail. "Before Agnes was killed, Adrian kept telling us every day that there is no sin in killing children because when they die, they will go to heaven; that we must not be afraid to do the killing because all the holy ones from the spiritual world, especially his Old Master, Pragngan and his soul, will be looking down on us, looking at what we do. Every day he kept telling us this while he was in a trance."

Mui Choo said she realised her folly and began to feel guilty only after her arrest and while Inspector Simon Suppiah was questioning her. She realised that Adrian was a fake and all his antics were mumbo-jumbo. Mui Choo denied portions in her police statement where she said that after she moved in with Adrian she realised that he was a fake. She told the court that right up to her arrest, she believed that he possessed supernatural powers, although she also believed that he tricked his clients into handing him their valuables. "At that time, when he was taking people's gold ornaments, I did not like it. But I could not tell him off because he said the spirits in him knew what he was doing and they could foretell the future," she said. Although she realised that he tricked his clients, she did not warn them about it. "I couldn't, because I was under his control," she said.

Cross-examined by Adrian's lawyer, Mr Howard Cashin, Mui Choo denied that she was already a prostitute when she met Adrian. "If I was a prostitute at that time, I wouldn't have been fooled by Adrian when he told me he had a weak heart and that there would be 'no sex, bodily contact only'. I would have known what 'bodily contact' with a man was. I would not have involved my own sister," she said. She may have been working in a bar, but she was ignorant about sex and never talked to the other bargirls about sex. When she met Adrian, he was polite, pleasant, friendly, smiling and happy. She liked him, but soon felt sorry for him when he told her that being a holy man, he would die young.

Sometime in 1974, Adrian started taking her out and told her he had a weak heart. When she finally agreed to have "bodily contact" with him at a flat in Pacific Mansions, they lay in bed naked, but did not have sexual intercourse. She agreed with Mr Cashin that she was so naive at the time that it did not occur to her that if she continued having such physical contact with Adrian, it would lead to intercourse. Adrian remained pleasant, outgoing and jovial. He never lost his temper and never forced her to do anything she did not want to do. She still liked and pitied him. By the middle of 1975, Adrian had begun suggesting that she should become a prostitute. She said she agreed eventually because she had come to believe that she was fated to be Adrian's "holy wife". He told her that if she became a prostitute, he would make all the arrangements, take her to the meeting places and fetch her home afterwards, and by doing all these things he would be showing her that he really loved and cared for her. "He's got a way of talking to you so that you fall into his trap," she said. "I'd never experienced love. I was very foolish at that time and I thought it was all true, that was how he loved me, by bringing me around."

Towards the end of 1975, after Mui Choo had moved into Adrian's Toa Payoh flat and his family had left, he stopped being nice all the time. He became irritable and temperamental. He quit his job as a bill collector, prepared his altar and set up his practice as a spirit medium and fortune-teller. Mui Choo continued working and handed him all her money – at least $100 a day from prostitution and $1,000 a month from her nighttime job as a bar waitress. Adrian stopped having sex with her and no longer chatted with her as he used to. By 1976, she had come to fear Adrian. She feared his trances and his talk of gods and spirits, and he had also begun beating her. They were now in show business too. Mui Choo said they did not eat well during this period because Adrian wanted to save money. The same year, Mui Choo's younger sister moved into the flat, became Adrian's "holy wife" and a prostitute. Mui Choo told the court Adrian had promised that he would not have intercourse with her sister and she believed him in spite of having been tricked herself. Asked why she believed him, Mui Choo replied: "Because when he gets into a trance and tells me all these things, I fear him, and when I get frightened, I go blank and I don't think." Mui Choo said she felt very sorry for her sister and was upset that Adrian had slept with them both, but she was not upset when her sister became a prostitute because she regarded it as a way of taking revenge against their father.

In June 1977, Adrian married Mui Choo at the Registry of Marriages. Mui Choo said she was confused about her feelings for Adrian, who did not make love to her but continued having sex with other women in their flat. When Mr Cashin asked why she married Adrian, she replied: "Because I was stuck already. After making my vows, I could not run away." She agreed with the lawyer that she had married Adrian despite his bad temper and moods, and despite the fact that he beat her, had forced her and her younger sister into prostitution, had not slept with her in three years and was now having sex with other women.

Questioned about the blood-drinking that went on at the flat, Mui Choo said Adrian spoke to the goddess Kali whenever he drank blood. Sometimes he brought chicken blood and made her drink it, saying it would get rid of her evil spirits. Mui Choo admitted that she sometimes pretended to be in a trance herself. Once, Adrian told her and a Malay girl, Ani, to concentrate on the goddess Kali at his altar. Ani went into a trance but Mui Choo did not. Adrian then splashed lime juice into her eyes and pumped it up her nose. To avoid further torture, she imitated Ani and pretended to be in a trance too. Mui Choo denied once again that Adrian told her she slept with her tongue sticking out and that he took her to several *bomoh*s to find a cure. He took her to some Hindu temples, she said, but it was because of her evil spirits, although it also had something to do with the goddess Kali. Adrian told her it was the evil spirits in her that enjoyed sex and that was the reason why he made her have sex with two young boys – a neighbour from their block and her teenaged brother.

Mui Choo said Adrian sometimes asked those who came to the flat to sit before his altar and look at the various idols and deities. Some people who did this would start to tremble. He would then say that they had been in a trance, although Mui Choo did not think so herself. She said it was not true that Kah Hong's mother and husband, Ah Hua, were spirit mediums as Adrian claimed. She could not recall

Ah Hua ever going into a trance and insulting the goddess Kali and the other deities, and Adrian never told her that he killed Ah Hua because he had insulted the gods. Mui Choo said she always believed that Ah Hua had died the way Adrian explained it – he was killed by Kah Hong's evil spirit. Mui Choo agreed with Mr Cashin that just before the child killings, she was subjected to more beatings and increased pressure from Adrian. He was angry more often and administered his electric shock treatments to her more frequently too.

Cross-examined by Kah Hong's lawyer, Mr Nathan Isaac, Mui Choo denied that she and Adrian worked as a team to cheat his clients. She said the people who came to the flat were impressed by Adrian and his gods. But she took part in his altar ceremonies, chanting verses, ringing a bell and lighting joss sticks, and played a major part in convincing Kah Hong of Adrian's powers by acting as the interpreter when he went into a trance and spoke in Malay. She agreed with Mr Isaac that Kah Hong regarded Adrian as being "almost god-like". Kah Hong became Adrian's "holy wife" after Mui Choo convinced her that all her problems with evil spirits would be solved if she was married in heaven to Adrian.

Mr Isaac then asked Mui Choo to confirm various incidents that took place after Kah Hong became Adrian's "holy wife". She said it was true that, at Adrian's instigation, Kah Hong returned to her mother's home and smashed the family altar and, on two occasions, assaulted her mother and two brothers at Adrian's flat. Because of Adrian's influence, Kah Hong treated Ah Hua very badly. Kah Hong did not cry on the night Ah Hua died but her behaviour changed in the weeks that followed. "She saw shadows at night, she heard voices … people telling her that her life was in danger … she was miserable." When Kah Hong told Adrian all this, he said it was just her evil spirits bothering her and gave her the electric shock treatment. Mui Choo said she later learnt from Adrian that Kah Hong had tried to kill herself and was admitted to Woodbridge Hospital. Mui Choo said she had never seen Kah Hong in a trance and did not know why Adrian told the court that Kah Hong was possessed by the Goddess of Hell. She maintained, as she said in her statement to the police, that Adrian had told her that Kah Hong was useful to them and if she became a nuisance, he would kill her. "I just listened with shock. Why did he want her as a holy wife and, at the same time, want to kill her? I just didn't understand."

DPP Glenn Knight began his cross-examination of Mui Choo by asking her about Adrian's so-called trances. Mui Choo said if Adrian could not persuade a woman to have sex with him, he would go into a trance, say he was possessed by the Old Master or Datuk Pragngan, and tell the woman that she was destined to become his "holy wife". That was how Adrian tricked Christina Chong. His needles-in-the-egg ruse convinced everybody every time and Mui Choo confessed that she had been fooled by it herself. Whenever Adrian had clients who seemed unsure about his supernatural powers, he performed the egg trick and it always worked. Mui Choo said she believed in his supernatural powers and sometimes spoke to those who doubted Adrian, convincing them of his powers. She said Adrian had a supernatural soul named Ah Liah or "Long Time No See", which travelled everywhere. Whenever Adrian assaulted her, he said it was Ah Liah who did it, although he sometimes blamed his Old Master or Datuk Pragngan. Mui Choo said: "I didn't know that his trances were fake." If she had known they were fake, she would have left Adrian.

Mr Knight: Your evidence is that Adrian was a very persuasive, kind and gentle person, and that is why he was able to convince everybody into doing various things, is that right? And that included you?

Mui Choo: Yes.

Mr Knight: And when you didn't do things he wanted you to do, he would go into a trance and assault you and you were prepared to live with him throughout this period because you thought it wasn't him but some other person assaulting you?

Mui Choo: Yes, out of fear.

Mr Knight: Because you thought it was somebody else who was doing it and not Adrian himself, is that right?

Mui Choo: Yes.

Mui Choo said she even believed Adrian's claim that the electric shock treatment was done to drive away evil spirits. Although she was afraid of it, complained to Adrian and even cried to avoid it, he would not stop the treatment. She did not tell anyone because "people would laugh at me and ask how could I accept it". Mui Choo said she had fallen for his story about his weak heart and believed that he was saving her earnings for surgery overseas. But whenever she asked him when he was going for his operation, he would say: "When the time comes." Mui Choo told the court that she now realised that Adrian's story about his weak heart was only a lie meant to keep her running around and working while he could stay at home relaxing, womanising and listening to music. She said she lived in fear of Adrian up to the day of her arrest. "Then the police told me that Adrian was a fake, and everything else about him – there were no supernatural powers, I was just an instrument for him."

Questioned about Adrian's work as a medium, Mui Choo said that he made things very dramatic to impress his clients. He would somersault or leap backwards suddenly to indicate the start or end of his trance to create the impression that something was entering or leaving his body. Sometimes he used a snake for extra effect. Adrian milked clients who donated big sums, by making them come back to see him again and again. But although the money kept pouring in, she said, Adrian was tight-fisted. It was not true that he kept the cash in a drawer for her and Kah Hong to help themselves whenever they liked. He told them that if they did anything without his knowledge, the gods would inform him. Adrian kept the key to the cash drawer, but near the end of 1980, she took $14,000 for her slimming treatment without telling him. She took Adrian's keys while he was asleep and helped herself to the cash.

Mr Knight then set out to show that Mui Choo was party to Adrian's crimes. She confirmed that she, Adrian and Kah Hong had agreed to kill Ghazali. It was true, too, that she and Kah Hong agreed to comply with Adrian's instruction to drug the boy so that it would be easier to kill him. Part of the plan, in both child killings, was that Mui Choo and Kah Hong would swallow empty capsules to encourage the children to swallow the real drugs. Each of them had a part to play in both killings. She could not recall discussing the disposal of the boy's body, but after Mr Knight referred her to her police statement, Mui Choo agreed that this was discussed while Ghazali slept. Although she was not afraid of being caught, Mui Choo helped to cover up the two murders. On Adrian's instructions, she cleaned the bag in which Agnes' body was disposed to make sure there were no fingerprints on it. After Ghazali's body had been dumped, she helped to remove some of the bloodstains leading to their flat. Although there had been a discussion about whether Ghazali should be killed, she and Kah Hong just listened while Adrian asked the questions and answered them himself. Mui Choo said it was Kah Hong who carried Ghazali's body out of the flat with Adrian that night, not her. As for Agnes, Mui Choo and Kah Hong gave the girl tranquillisers while Adrian peeped to see if the girl was suitable for sexual intercourse. Mui Choo also took the girl into the back room and talked about cosmetics before bringing her out into the hall again.

When Mr Knight began questioning her about the many other women in Adrian's life, Mui Choo said she only knew his instruction that she should not obstruct him in whatever he did with the women. "I did obstruct once, and I was hit for it. Because of this, I feared him," she said. That occasion was when she discovered that Adrian had broken his word and had sexual intercourse with her teenaged sister. She was furious, but she let him continue having sex with her sister because he went into a trance, hit her and asked why she was being so selfish when he had a weak heart. He asked if she was trying to kill him.

Mr Knight asked Mui Choo if she really hated her father so much that she could accept Adrian's suggestion that her younger sister should become a prostitute as a form of revenge against their father. "Yes, because Adrian had been putting poison in my head that my father hated me and my mother hated me; he knew that my parents did not love me. He kept telling me that my parents were casting spells on me and that made me hate them," she said. When Mr Knight asked what supernatural powers she thought Adrian possessed, she replied: "He could read people's thoughts. He knew whatever I was thinking; he could see the future, he could tell whether the future was good or bad for me. He said he knew and that he could see evil spirits in my body."

Mr Knight then questioned Mui Choo about her role in getting women to have sex with Adrian. She agreed that she encouraged some of them to become Adrian's "holy wives" and that she told others that they would remain young and pretty forever if they had sex with him. But she maintained that she only did these things because Adrian had warned her not to block his dealings with other women.

Mr Knight pointed out that she had in fact done much more – she had encouraged and induced people to believe various things. Agreeing, she said: "At that time I did not know what I was doing was wrong." She had encouraged Christina Chong to become Adrian's "holy wife" and helped her to become a prostitute. Asked why she never warned Christina, Mui Choo replied: "I could not because Adrian made me believe that he could read people's minds. I always thought that he had his Old Master and Datuk Pragngan with him and he could see what I was doing." She knew that Adrian was deceiving people, and she fooled the women herself, but she insisted that she only did this because she was afraid he would beat her.

Mui Choo: Before Christina came, I wanted to leave him but he wouldn't let me go. After Christina went back to Kuala Lumpur, again I told him I wanted to leave him. I even went to the extreme and told him that I could not stand the sight of him. He still would not let me go. He told me it was only the evil controlling me. He kept telling me throughout that he would only let me go when the time came … I even gave him the idea that I could go and drown myself in the sea, but he still wouldn't let me go.

Mr Knight: Was Adrian Lim in love with you?

Mui Choo: No.

Mr Knight: He didn't love you?

Mui Choo: No.

Mr Knight: And you didn't love him?

Mui Choo: No.

Questioned by Mr Knight about her trances, Mui Choo said she once faked a trance, by moving and shaking her body, to prove to Christina that the goddess Kali could enter her body. Although it was not a very good act, Christina was convinced. Mui Choo admitted that the act was also meant to help Adrian get money from Christina. Asked to elaborate on Adrian's tight-fistedness, she said: "He wouldn't allow me to go shopping. There were no occasions to celebrate, not even Christmas or Chinese New Year, nothing." But she helped Adrian to take valuables from his clients and helped him to cheat them. If a client accidentally touched her while Adrian was praying, he would demand that Mui Choo be given a *hongbao* because she was pure. She would usually collect red packets containing between $30 and $50.

Justice Sinnathuray: He tells them that they get cured when they touch you and so they have to give you a *hongbao*?

Mui Choo: Yes.

Justice Sinnathuray: You knew that couldn't be correct, didn't you? Couldn't be true, could it? By touching you, someone else couldn't be cured, could he?

Mui Choo: Yes.

Justice Sinnathuray: By taking the *hongbao*, you know that is fraud, that is cheating, isn't it?

Mui Choo: Yes.

Mr Knight: Mui Choo, the truth is, is it not, that you knew that he was a fake all along?

Mui Choo: No. Cheating, yes. But I always believed he had spiritual power.

Mr Knight: You knew he was cheating and using deception, yes, so you accept him as a fake for that. But you don't accept him as a fake for spiritual powers?

Mui Choo: Yes.

Mr Knight: Even though he used both at the same time?

Mui Choo: That's why, when he used both at the same time, I was very confused. I just didn't understand … Although I could see it was not right, I could not make out in my own mind why one part was real, one part was fake.

Mui Choo said she did not do any regular work from 1980. She never stopped being a prostitute, but only went out if a pimp telephoned for her services. There were few calls in 1979, none in 1980 and one in 1981, just before Agnes' murder. She never knew how much money Adrian had in the flat, although she saw him counting the cash. She clarified that she did not remove the $14,000 for her slimming treatment all at once, but took $1,000 at a time. She also spent "a few thousand dollars" on cosmetics in 1980 and those big purchases earned her the privilege of house calls from beautician Lucy Lau. Mui Choo disagreed with Mr Knight's suggestion that she frightened Lucy Lau into having sex with Adrian. When Mr Knight told her he did not believe that she did things only on Adrian's instructions, Mui Choo replied: "If he is my husband, why would I want to see him having sex with another woman in front of my eyes? Why should I suffer from that?" Mr Knight reminded Mui Choo that she had told the court that she did not love Adrian, but in her police statement, she had said she was jealous of the women he slept with.

Mr Knight: Why were you jealous?
Mui Choo: I could not control him.
Mr Knight: You could not control him? Did you
    want to control him?
Mui Choo: Yes.
Mr Knight: You wanted him for yourself?
Mui Choo: Yes.

When Mr Knight returned to questioning her about Lucy Lau, Mui Choo agreed that Adrian had, in effect, raped the beautician because he frightened her into believing that if she did not have sex with him, evil spirits would enter her body. Recalling the incident when Adrian was assaulted at Lucy Lau's house, Mui Choo said: "He was so afraid that he pushed me in front of him and let me get assaulted by those men. I was so shocked and confused. I wondered how come, in our house, he could threaten me and talk so big about himself, but in front of people he turned so small, like a mouse? I just didn't believe it anymore."

Mr Knight: Are you trying to tell us that he was a coward as well?

Mui Choo: Yes … that was the only time that I saw the whole picture.

Even then, Mui Choo dared not confront Adrian. She said it did not strike her that cowardice lay behind Adrian's decision to kill children, not adults. Nor did it occur to her that he really did not have any powers to see into the future as he had not predicted the assault. After Adrian was charged with rape and she was charged with helping him commit the crime, Adrian told her and Kah Hong to give the police false statements. Mui Choo said the statement she made to the police was a recitation of what Adrian had told her to say. Mr Knight referred to the five-page statement she gave to the police on the rape case and commented that it was a clear and lengthy account which did not suggest that she was confused. But she said: "It was all on Adrian's instructions."

When the DPP returned to the subject of Adrian's tricks, Mui Choo said she saw the needles-in-the-egg trick only twice: once when Adrian performed it for Christina and the other time, for Kah Hong's sister. She said she learnt the truth about the egg trick only after her arrest, after Adrian had shown the police how he did it. Mui Choo said she knew that Adrian bought drugs from doctors and dispensed them to his clients, but she thought he proved his supernatural powers by prescribing the right drugs to the right clients. Mui Choo maintained that she did not know that this was fake because "he made it look real all the time". She denied that she worked with Adrian as a team in tricking people. She admitted that she sometimes faked being in a trance herself, but she said she did it out of fear of the electric shock treatment.

> **Mr Knight**: There were times when you fooled him, weren't there?
>
> **Mui Choo**: Yes.
>
> **Mr Knight**: How could you fool the Old Master?
>
> **Mui Choo**: I don't know. I did it out of fear.
>
> **Mr Knight**: Out of fear, you fooled him?
>
> **Mui Choo**: Yes.
>
> **Mr Knight**: And he was fooled! Mui Choo, I have to put it to you that you yourself knew that Adrian had no supernatural powers.
>
> **Mui Choo**: I did not know at that time.
>
> **Justice Sinnathuray**: Is it your evidence now that

you can't understand why you did all these
multitudinous things for him?

Mui Choo: Yes.

Mr Knight: My case, Mui Choo, is that everything
that you did was done deliberately.

Mui Choo: Because he had a way of convincing and
persuading people to do it …

Mr Knight: So he convinced you, persuaded you,
and you agreed to what he wanted you to do and
then you did it?

Mui Choo: Yes.

When Mr Knight referred to her show business career,
Mui Choo said she had been forced by Adrian to be a
stripper. He scolded her and humiliated her if she did not
dance in step with the music. Shown a publicity photograph
of her and Adrian, Mr Knight asked how someone who was
confused and frightened and who did not like the job could
smile for the camera. She replied: "I had to smile because I
was taking a photograph."

Mr Knight then referred Mui Choo to testimony by
Christina Chong and Adrian, who both said that she never
seemed to mind the electric shock treatment. Mui Choo said
she could not show her fear to Christina as Adrian would
torture her even more afterwards. Mui Choo agreed that
she had put on an act for Christina. She was also jealous of
Christina and Kah Hong, but could not show it. She agreed
with Mr Knight that she put on an act for every woman in

Adrian's love life, pretending that she did not mind. But by August or September 1980, she felt that she just could not tolerate Adrian any longer. She agreed with Mr Knight that she joined the slimming centre and spent a great deal on cosmetics because she was concerned about her looks. She was a woman who liked wearing nice clothes too. "At that time, he kept saying that I was ugly and he would give me more shock treatment, saying evil was controlling part of my face, I looked ugly, my eyes were evil. That's why I turned to personal beauty."

When Mr Knight asked about the huge stocks of drugs at the flat, Mui Choo admitted that she had misled the two doctors into giving her more medicine than she needed. She said Adrian told her he was going to Europe for medical treatment and needed to stock up on the drugs. But Mui Choo knew that Adrian sold the drugs to some of his clients and handed them out whenever he performed his electric shock treatment. Mui Choo said it became a habit for her to take the pills every night. After Kah Hong came out of Woodbridge Hospital in mid-1980, Adrian hid her psychiatric medicines and would decide when to give some to Mui Choo and Kah Hong. She could not refuse to take the medicines because Adrian would watch her swallow them. He did not force them down her throat, but insisted that she take them because they were good for her. The medicines made her feel "sleepy, tired, heavy and stupid".

Mr Knight asked her why she wanted to see a psychiatrist after Kah Hong came out of Woodbridge Hospital. Mui

Choo replied that she felt that if something was wrong with Kah Hong, something had to be wrong with her, too. "I knew something was wrong with me, that's all ... I realised I wasn't living, I was only existing. I was no more the happy person, I had no life in me any more," she said.

Mui Choo admitted that although she continued to see Dr Yeo Peng Ngee throughout 1980, she never told him about her thoughts of suicide or her feelings of confusion. Mr Knight said he believed she never felt any of these things at all, but Mui Choo maintained that they were all true. Mui Choo claimed that she never told anyone that she saw visions of a pumpkin-like creature after Ah Hua's death, because nobody had asked her about them. Questioned about her claim that she also heard the sound of beating gongs after Ah Hua's death, Mui Choo conceded that the sound might have come from a temple near the Toa Payoh flat.

Mui Choo told the court there were no rituals performed when the two children were killed. There were no prayers, no lighting of joss sticks and no ringing of bells. It was not true that Adrian was praying at the altar when Agnes and Ghazali were brought into the flat. She did not know why Adrian decided to snip off some of Ghazali's hair and throw it under the living room sofa.

Winding up his cross-examination, Mr Knight told Mui Choo he believed that she, Adrian and Kah Hong killed the two children to distract the police from investigating Lucy Lau's rape report. She replied: "I did it because Adrian instructed me. I had no intention of confusing the police."

Mr Knight said he also believed that she was in full control of herself throughout the killings, that Adrian, Mui Choo and Kah Hong worked as a team, and that Mui Choo knew quite well that what she was doing was wrong. Mui Choo denied it all.

Before Mr Jeyaretnam began his re-examination of his client, Justice Sinnathuray asked Mui Choo why, when the charges had been read out to her earlier, she admitted killing the two children. She replied: "That is because I did it."

> **Mr Jeyaretnam**: The court is concerned with her mental responsibility for her physical act.
>
> **Justice Sinnathuray**: So far as the second accused is concerned, she admits to the killings.
>
> **Mr Jeyaretnam**: Yes, the physical …
>
> **Justice Sinnathuray**: No, no, not only the physical acts but her mental state in doing the killings. She knew what she was doing, but the question is, was she suffering from an abnormality of the mind?
>
> **Mr Jeyaretnam**: If she didn't know what she was doing, then we would be handing a defence of insanity. Our defence is simply this: Can she be held fully responsible mentally?

Mr Jeyaretnam took Mui Choo through a number of points which had been raised during cross-examination.

Asked what she did when Adrian had women at the flat, Mui Choo said she would walk along the streets or window shop. She said she never told Dr Yeo Peng Ngee her problems because she did not know how to speak to him and felt that he never really showed much concern even when she was ill. "If you tell him you have bone aches, he will just prescribe the medicine. He'll never ask you how you got it." She did not tell the doctor about the electric shock treatments either. "I dared not tell him. I was afraid of Adrian," she said.

Mui Choo still maintained that there had been no rituals when the two children were killed. There was blood drinking on both nights and blood was connected with Kali, but Mui Choo said Adrian told her to drink blood to drive out her evil spirits. It never occurred to her that if she obstructed Adrian, he would kill her and she would get to die as she wished. If she obstructed him, she said, "he would either beat me up or give me the shock treatments". She also maintained that she believed Adrian throughout their elaborate joint suicide attempt. It never occurred to her that it was all a charade and that he had removed the contents of the capsules they swallowed.

CHAPTER 12

HOE KAH HONG: "ADRIAN'S JUST A COCKROACH NOW"

Hoe Kah Hong thought Adrian Lim was a god the first time she saw him in action before his altar. When her husband died during Adrian's electric shock treatment, she believed Adrian that an evil spirit in her had jumped out and killed him. She said it was only after her arrest that she realised Adrian had fooled her.

Hoe Kah Hong was 25 years old and had known Adrian Lim for slightly over a year when she found herself arrested together with him and his wife Tan Mui Choo for murdering two children. Her mother had taken her to Adrian's Toa Payoh flat in late 1979 because of her bad temper and outbursts at home. Although legally married to Benson Loh Ngak Hua and preparing to celebrate their customary Chinese wedding, Kah Hong soon became Adrian's "holy wife" and started having sex with him. Within months, in January 1980, her husband Ah Hua was dead, electrocuted while undergoing one of Adrian's electric shock treatments. A year later, after Adrian had been accused of raping beautician Lucy Lau, Kah Hong did as he asked and brought five children to the flat. They included Agnes Ng Siew Heok and Ghazali Marzuki who were killed.

At the trial, Kah Hong spent four days in the witness stand when her turn came to present her defence. Examined by her lawyer, Mr Nathan Isaac, she said she never knew the truth about Ah Hua's death until after her arrest. Adrian had told her that the evil spirit in her had jumped out and killed Ah Hua, and she believed this all along. It was only while she was being questioned by Inspector Simon Suppiah at the CID that she realised she did not know how Ah Hua died. She told the court that Adrian was brought to her and she questioned him. "I asked him whether he was the one who killed Ah Hua. He said yes. I asked him whether he raped Lucy Lau. He said yes. I asked him whether he was god or devil. He said he didn't know." Kah Hong had come a long way from the first time she set eyes on Adrian in 1979 and she thought he was a god when he went into a trance in front of his altar. She burst out laughing and told the court: "It sounds ridiculous. He had a lot of tricks."

Adrian tricked her into believing that she had an evil spirit in her. He tricked her into undergoing his electric shock treatments. She was hooded the first time he applied his electric shock device on her and had no idea what was going on. "I seemed to see spirits moving about," she told the court.

Throughout the session, Mui Choo chanted while Adrian berated the spirits in her and ordered them to get out of her body. Then he pumped lemon juice up Kah Hong's nose, and as the smarting pain hit her, she saw lights, trembled and felt weak. Adrian then declared that he had driven out her evil spirits. He tricked Kah Hong into staying at the Toa Payoh flat for her own good by warning her that two more spirits were waiting for her outside. She moved in and stayed three months, during which Adrian tricked her into becoming his "holy wife" and she began having sex with him.

Kah Hong moved out of the flat after Ah Hua's death on 7 January 1980 because Adrian did not want to arouse any suspicion that he was having an affair with the dead man's wife. She moved to a rented room in Clementi, but became unhappy and withdrawn. Kah Hong told the court that she began hearing voices telling her when Mui Choo was washing clothes at the Toa Payoh flat or when Adrian woke up. She started smoking and drinking liquor. Then a voice began telling her to swallow insecticide. "It was an inner voice and I kept thinking of insecticide. After work, I would walk up and down inside the flat and I kept seeing insecticide. I told Adrian that I kept thinking of drinking insecticide, and he said, 'Carry on, take three cups.'" She swallowed some insecticide. It made her vomit blood, but she did not go to hospital.

Another time, a voice told her to bang her head against the wall, and again, when she told Adrian, he told her to go ahead and do it. She did, and injured her shoulder. Kah

Hong recalled a day when Adrian took her on his motorcycle to MacRitchie Reservoir and they met with an accident. She hurt her hand and needed treatment in hospital. She told the court that she now realised that Adrian had intended to kill her that day. Apart from hearing voices, Kah Hong said she had visions too. "I saw spirits moving about and I followed them. I heard voices calling my name." Whenever she was at a high place, a voice would tell her to jump. When she told Adrian, he said she must have several evil spirits in her. One day she woke up and found herself in Alexandra Hospital. She was told she had swallowed a large quantity of pills and a neighbour had brought her to hospital.

Kah Hong was transferred to Woodbridge Hospital where she remained for 45 days. She telephoned Adrian often while she was warded there, but he never came to visit. He cautioned her against eating any food brought by her mother, saying her mother had cast an evil spell on her. Kah Hong went to the Toa Payoh flat as soon as she was allowed weekends off from hospital, and after she was discharged. Adrian took away her medicines saying his Old Master had said the pills would be good for him. She went back to Woodbridge twice in 10 days to get him more, lying each time that she had lost her medicines. Adrian fed her sedatives instead of the medicines the hospital psychiatrists had prescribed.

Kah Hong said that when she returned to her room in Clementi, she continued seeing visions, including that of Ah Hua dressed in yellow robes. She also saw a figure lurking behind her bed at night, and it would always disappear by daylight. Her suicidal thoughts persisted. By September 1980, she would go to the Toa Payoh flat twice a week and during those visits she would have sex with Adrian and undergo the electric shock treatment. When she complained of seeing evil spirits, Adrian told her she was the devil and so it was natural for her to see evil spirits. Adrian and Mui Choo took her to a Hindu temple in Serangoon Road several times and, Kah Hong said, she would spend a long time gazing into the eyes of the statue of goddess Kali. "Adrian said that if I felt like crying, I should cry, and if I felt like bowing, I should do so, and then the evil spirits would go out. I swept the temple floor. He said it was the evil spirit in me that made me sweep the floor," she said.

One day Adrian telephoned Kah Hong and asked her to come to the flat right away because his time was up. Kah Hong told the court she was so happy to hear that because she wanted to die with him too. To prepare herself for death, she painted her fingernails red and wore a red dress. When she reached Toa Payoh, she found that Christina Chong had also been summoned from Kuala Lumpur. Kah Hong was disappointed when Adrian told her she could not join him and Mui Choo in their joint suicide. She protested and insisted that she wanted to die too. Adrian then handed her a pair of dice and asked her to toss them and see if it was her time to die as well. "When the dice fell, he said the answer was no. There was no choice," she said. Adrian gave her a thick wad of cash and a note which, he said, bequeathed the flat to her. Kah Hong and Christina watched as Adrian and Mui Choo swallowed a massive number of pills and fell asleep – but they did not die.

Kah Hong told the court that at the end of 1980, Adrian called her and complained that Lucy Lau had filed a rape report against him. Kah Hong said she asked him if the allegation was true, and he cried as he denied it. She said that she felt sorry for him and agreed to lie to the police that she had been with Adrian on every occasion that Lucy Lau came to the flat. She said Adrian was angry with the police and wanted to take revenge over the rape report. Kah Hong's lawyer, Mr Nathan Isaac, asked her what kind of revenge Adrian had in mind and she replied: "He said he wanted to catch and kill children. When they were killed, they would go to heaven." He also said the goddess Kali would approve of these killings.

Mr Isaac referred Kah Hong to the deaths of Agnes and Ghazali, and asked how the children had been killed. Kah Hong said: "I caught hold of Agnes' head and pushed it into the tub which was full of water. I used both my hands and pushed her head down. Adrian stepped on Agnes' back with one foot to hold her head down and Mui Choo held the legs." Adrian then electrocuted Agnes. The two women dried and dressed the dead child's body before stuffing her into the bag, and all three took it out of the flat. Less than a fortnight later, Kah Hong picked Ghazali to take to the flat. When Justice Sinnathuray asked why she chose a boy, Kah Hong replied: "Ghazali's face looked like my husband's face." She could not recall the details of Ghazali's death. She remembered Adrian carrying the boy into the bathroom. Late that night, Kah Hong said, she carried the body out of the flat and left it outside a block. Adrian accompanied her and held a handkerchief at the boy's nose as it was dripping blood. Afterwards, all three went out to clean the bloodstains. Kah Hong said she was angry when the police turned up at the flat after Ghazali's body was found. "I thought we were not in the wrong and no offence had been committed," she said.

After her arrest, Kah Hong discovered the various ways in which Adrian had tricked her. She told the court she refused to believe Inspector Suppiah and Inspector Richard Pereira when they revealed that Adrian's apparent ability to draw needles out of people's bodies was only a trick. She turned to Mui Choo, who confirmed what the detectives had said. "I hated Mui Choo then," said Kah Hong. Inspector Suppiah had brought along some amulets. He placed them on the floor and asked Adrian to step on them to prove that they were all false. Adrian did so. Justice Sinnathuray asked Kah Hong if she still believed that Adrian had some supernatural powers. She laughed and replied: "No, not now. Now he is a cockroach."

Mr Isaac asked Kah Hong about the abuse she had suffered at Adrian's hands. She said Adrian had been nice to her, but he also beat her and made her undergo his electric shock treatment more than 50 times. He once slapped and kicked her because she had forgotten to take her contraceptive pills. He kicked her stomach repeatedly until she vomited. Another time, she fainted after he tried to strangle her with a strip of cloth. On other occasions, he pulled her hair, banged her head against the wall, kicked her head and pinched her stomach until it became blue-black.

Adrian's lawyer, Mr Howard Cashin, was next to question Kah Hong. He asked if she had known that Adrian was married to Mui Choo before she started having sex with him. She replied that although she thought it was wrong to steal another woman's husband, it was Adrian who told her to sleep with him. "He wanted to possess me. He knew I was a virgin," she said. He also told her that the sex god, Datuk Pragngan, wanted to have sex with her. Kah Hong said that whenever Adrian wanted to have sex with her, he would tell Mui Choo to leave the flat and telephone before returning. Kah Hong said Mui Choo looked depressed, as if she did not like what was going on, but she had to do whatever Adrian told her.

Mr Cashin asked: "Do you think there was anything morally wrong with having sex with another woman's husband?" Kah Hong replied: "Adrian said that he did not want Mui Choo anymore. He told me once that Mui Choo was too fat. Adrian told me I was fated to sleep with him, and Mui Choo was fated to kill and destroy the devils or evil spirits."

Mr Cashin questioned her about bringing children to the flat. She said that after Adrian was charged with rape, he became aggressive and talked about taking revenge against the police by killing children. The way she understood it, the goddess Kali wanted the children killed, and Datuk Pragngan wanted them raped before death. Adrian also told her that if she brought him children, she would not have to undergo the electric shock treatments. On the five occasions that she brought children to the flat, she was spared the electric shock treatment. But on the days when she was unsuccessful, Adrian pumped lemon juice up her nose and beat her. Kah Hong maintained that she thought she was doing the right thing when she helped in the child killings, because she believed in the goddess Kali. Although she lost faith in Adrian after her arrest, she said she still believed in goddess Kali and Datuk Pragngan.

Questioned next by Mr J.B. Jeyaretnam, counsel for Mui Choo, Kah Hong said Mui Choo was just as terrified as she was of the electric shock treatment. "When she was frightened, she would say she did not like the electric shocks. But when she refused it, Adrian would say that evil spirits were controlling her mind." Kah Hong also said it was quite some time after she became his "holy wife" that he told her he no longer desired Mui Choo. "Adrian told me that Mui Choo was locked up," she said. Justice Sinnathuray asked what that meant. Mr Isaac said something to Mr Jeyaretnam, who told the judge: "She was locked up … I suppose, sexually locked up, frigid."

When Mr Jeyaretnam completed his cross-examination, Justice Sinnathuray remarked: "There is so much conflicting evidence in this case and when you try to look at it in relation to other witnesses, it is also conflicting. But the essential facts of this case are not in dispute."

*

It was DPP Glenn Knight's turn to question Kah Hong and before he started, he wanted her long statement to the police read back to her. Mr Isaac was concerned to hear this and told the court: "Sometimes with this witness, when suggestions are put to her and dragged back, she might agree."

But Justice Sinnathuray replied: "Well, Mr Isaac, that's the point. That's the whole object of our system, isn't it? Giving evidence in chief, then being cross-examined and re-examined to decide how much weight one can put on the evidence – that's how the system is."

The statement was read back to Kah Hong, and she told the court that everything she said in it was the truth.

Mr Knight asked Kah Hong what happened after Lucy Lau made a rape report against Adrian. Kah Hong said she went to the Toa Payoh flat immediately after Mui Choo called to inform her that Adrian had been arrested and was being held at the Toa Payoh Police Station. When Mui Choo told her that Adrian had been assaulted by some of Lucy's family members, she was filled with pity for him. Kah Hong said she went with Mui Choo to the police station to post bail for Adrian. When he saw the women, Adrian cried and told them he wanted to die. Adrian and Mui Choo went through their mock suicide attempt the following night. Asked by Mr Knight if she thought the so-called suicide bid was only a charade to impress Christina Chong, Adrian's "holy wife" from Kuala Lumpur, Kah Hong replied: "I should think so."

Mr Knight asked Kah Hong about the three months she stayed at the Toa Payoh flat before her husband Ah Hua's death. Kah Hong said Adrian treated her well except when he was in a trance and would beat her. She said he sometimes made Mui Choo assault her to get rid of the evil spirits in her. She agreed with Mr Knight that she obeyed the instructions Adrian gave her while he was in a trance. She said she would not have endured his beatings or the electric shock treatment if she did not believe his trances were real. That was also why she beat her mother with a broom, poured urine over her mother's head and assaulted her brothers when they came to Adrian's flat to persuade her to return home.

Justice Sinnathuray asked Kah Hong when, exactly, she stopped believing in Adrian's supernatural powers. She said it was while she was at the CID after her arrest that she realised that everything Adrian had told her about evil spirits dwelling in her was false. But she still believed he had some special powers. "He was still chanting prayers at the CID, so I thought he still had power," she said. She told the court that she still felt a little afraid of Adrian. She explained that ancestral worship had long been part of her family life, and she believed in the existence of good and bad spirits and the spirits of the dead.

Mr Knight questioned her about the death of her husband, Ah Hua. Kah Hong broke down and wept. She denied that she knew all along that Ah Hua had been electrocuted by Adrian, and it was not that an evil spirit had jumped out of her and killed him. "Had I known that, I would not have allowed myself to be given those electric shocks,' she said. She recalled that Adrian gave her strict instructions to cry whenever the police and Ah Hua's family members arrived at the flat, and to tell police that he was electrocuted by a faulty fan. "Adrian threatened me, saying if I didn't tell them what he told me to say, I might have to go to jail and he would also have to apply the electric shocks to me," she said.

Kah Hong was subdued as she related how she moved out of the Toa Payoh flat after Ah Hua's death. Mr Knight disputed her earlier testimony that she heard voices after she moved to a rented room in Clementi. But Kah Hong maintained that she heard voices and saw strange shadows too. When Mr Knight accused her of exaggerating, she replied: "This is the truth." Referring to her 45-day stay at Woodbridge Hospital, Mr Knight noted that she told psychiatrists that Ah Hua had been electrocuted by a faulty fan and that she cried a lot when talking about his death. Kah Hong agreed that she kept up the lie about the faulty fan and said nothing to the psychiatrists about the electric shock treatments. "I wouldn't dare to," she said. Justice Sinnathuray asked her: "Why? Were you afraid of Adrian Lim?" Kah Hong, who was crying, did not answer. The judge adjourned the day's hearing a little earlier than usual, noting that Kah Hong had been testifying all day.

When Mr Knight resumed his questioning, Kah Hong told the court that although she was unable to sleep, felt depressed and heard voices after Ah Hua died in January 1980, it was not until March that year that she told her company doctor about these problems. She agreed with Mr Knight that her depression was brought on by Ah Hua's death, and that her insomnia and anxiety in March were caused by the impending coroner's inquiry into his death. She was worried because she would have to repeat the lie about the faulty fan. Mr Knight noted that in 10 follow-up visits to Woodbridge Hospital, from 16 July 1980 to 31 January 1981, Kah Hong was cheerful and alert and told doctors she was no longer depressed. Even on 31 January 1981, a week after Agnes was killed, she had no complaints and told the doctor she was sleeping well. When Mr Knight pointed out that she never told the psychiatrists anything about goddess Kali, she replied: "I forgot to tell them."

Mr Knight moved on to the child killings. Kah Hong agreed that before each killing, Adrian held a discussion with her and Mui Choo on what to do with the child. There were no rituals involved in Ghazali's death, except that Adrian drank Ghazali's blood and the two women licked up the blood that remained in his cup. With Agnes, the three of them had only sucked blood from her pricked finger. Mr Knight disputed her earlier testimony that she picked Ghazali because he resembled Ah Hua and she now agreed that it had nothing to do with that. Mr Knight asked if she took part in the killings because she loved Adrian. "I loved him. I was also afraid of him," she replied. Then she added: "Actually, I did not love him. I loved the deities that he had and I thought that after I died, I would go to Buddha's world." She agreed with Mr Knight that she, Adrian and Mui Choo planned to kill the children, and that all three took part in killing them according to their plan. But she insisted that she did not know the killings were wrong because Adrian kept saying the children would go straight to heaven.

> **Justice Sinnathuray**: But to kill a child is something wrong, isn't it? To kill a human being is wrong.
> **Kah Hong**: But the children have gone to heaven.
> **Justice Sinnathuray**: All right.

Mr Isaac wrapped up by asking Kah Hong whom she thought she was protecting when she lied to the police about the circumstances of Ah Hua's death. At first she said she did not know. Then she said: "Myself." She said she was also protecting herself when she lied to her psychiatrists about Ah Hua's death. She was afraid to tell the truth because she still believed that her evil spirit killed him. She also believed that Adrian could read her mind. "For example, when I was watching TV and I did not know what I was thinking about, he knew. He would tell me not to think," she said. Asked why she never told anyone about the electric shock treatments, Kah Hong replied: "Even if I told anyone, no one would understand. They might think I was mad." She also said Adrian was always giving her instructions, directions and orders. "I never disagreed," she said. "Whatever he told me to do, I did it."

CHAPTER 13

WERE THEY MENTALLY ILL, OR WEREN'T THEY?

To escape death by hanging, Adrian Lim, Tan Mui Choo and Hoe Kah Hong had to persuade the trial judges that each was suffering from a serious mental illness when they killed Agnes Ng Siew Heok and Ghazali Marzuki. Psychiatric evidence was therefore a critical part of the trial, but the expert witnesses disagreed completely in their assessments of the mental state of the three killers.

Adrian Lim, Tan Mui Choo and Hoe Kah Hong did not dispute the overwhelming evidence DPP Glenn Knight put before the court to show that they killed Agnes Ng Siew Heok and Ghazali Marzuki. But all three hoped to avoid the death sentence by persuading Justice T. S. Sinnathuray and Justice F. A. Chua that they ought to be convicted of manslaughter, not murder. To do this, they had to show that at the time of the killings, each was suffering from a serious abnormality of the mind that diminished their mental responsibility for their actions.

A significant portion of the trial was devoted to hearing the views of psychiatrists who examined the three accused. The psychiatrists testifying for the defence presented a case of severe mental illness for each of the accused. Kah Hong, who spent 45 days at Woodbridge Hospital in 1980, also put in a defence of insanity. But Dr Chee Kuan Tsee of Woodbridge Hospital testified for the prosecution and presented the court with quite a different assessment, saying he was convinced that Adrian, Mui Choo and Kah Hong were not of unsound mind at the time of the killings.

ADRIAN LIM

Dr Wong Yip Chong, a senior psychiatrist in private practice, told the court that Adrian had manic depressive illness, a severe mental abnormality which causes the person to swing sharply between moods of elation and depression. He said Adrian killed Agnes and Ghazali while in a heightened state of his illness, during which he also suffered delusions about the Hindu goddess Kali. While in the elated or manic state, the patient is typically cheerful, talkative, jovial, energetic, lively and active most of the time, and his sexual activity would also be unusually increased. While in this state, the patient could also be domineering and irritable, and could suffer thought disorders, delusions and hallucinations, usually of a religious nature. Dr Wong said a psychologically stressful event could bring on an acute manic attack, which would usually last about two to three months. Such an attack is usually preceded by a period of depression, during which the patient feels sad, dejected and miserable, and might even attempt suicide.

Dr Wong felt Adrian fit the bill as a manic depressive. Adrian had been an extrovert and an active man who enjoyed company, was cheerful and talkative. He had a friendly personality, liked jokes and enjoyed good food, wine, women and song. The darker side of his personality was that he could be irritable, domineering and somewhat suspicious of others. Dr Wong thought Adrian crossed the line, from being a generally well-adjusted and well-regarded family man to a victim of a serious mental disorder sometime after 1974, when he immersed himself in the occult. From then until November 1980, when beautician Lucy Lau filed a rape report against him, Adrian's manic illness became increasingly apparent from his marked irritability, hypersexuality, an increasing tendency to dominate and his desire for religious power.

The psychological blow that triggered his acute manic episode was the rape report at the end of 1980. Adrian was depressed just before the onset of the manic state, Dr Wong said, pointing to evidence that Adrian cried after his arrest and his joint suicide bid with Mui Choo. As with other manic depressives, it was the people closest to Adrian who suffered the most and in silence because of his mental disease. His philandering, deceit and irritability were all features of the disease, as were his psychopathic tendencies, including his aggressive behaviour and domineering tendencies, and his paranoid tendencies, as when he believed that other people wanted to harm him. As for delusions, Dr Wong pointed out that at the height of his illness, Adrian firmly believed in the goddess Kali and that he was her specially chosen one. But as time went by after the killings, Adrian recovered from his illness and his religious delusions waned. That explained why Adrian told the court that the goddess Kali was a "puzzle" to him now. Adrian's spiritual motive for killing – as a form of sacrifice to the goddess – was consistent with the delusions he suffered at the height of his illness, said Dr Wong.

Adrian had given two other reasons for killing the children: he wanted to distract the police from investigating the rape report, and he wanted to take revenge against the police for all the trouble they caused him over the rape report. Dr Wong said these were irrational reasons. If Adrian really wanted to distract the police, he would have got someone else to do the killing; he would not have picked a victim like Agnes, from so near his home. He would have disposed of the bodies much further away from his flat, and he would have caused a crime which would not have brought such dire consequences for himself if he was caught. As for the revenge motive, Dr Wong said vengeance and anger usually lead to immediate, if not impulsive, crimes of violence usually directed at the original source of anger. Adrian had no history of impulsive violence and the child victims were totally unrelated to his trouble with the police.

Whatever anger Adrian felt would have dissipated during his long periods of meditation at his altar. Adrian had said that his meditation always left him feeling "strange and nice" – a state which Dr Wong said was incompatible with violence of this magnitude in a normal mind. Even if the killings had been acts of planned revenge, the slipshod disposal of the bodies was a telling point – if Adrian had been of a normal state of mind, it would have been obvious to him that he would face more trouble with the law, not less. For all these reasons, Dr Wong found Adrian's motives for the killings to be largely, if not totally, consistent with a person of abnormal mind and that the abnormality arose from manic depressive disease.

Dr Wong faced intense cross-examination by DPP Glenn Knight, who rejected the diagnosis. Dr Wong and Mr Knight were locked in disagreement for two days with the DPP contending that Adrian was not suffering from manic depressive disease at the time of the child killings, while Dr Wong remained steadfast by his diagnosis. When Mr Knight suggested that Dr Wong had merely strung together various factors to show that Adrian was mentally ill while ignoring those which indicated that he was not, the psychiatrist insisted that he had done a proper psychiatric evaluation. "If you don't put together what should be put together, then you are missing the diagnosis," he said. What was important was the overall picture, he stressed. "Otherwise, psychiatric symptoms taken one by one would have no meaning at all. Nobody would be mentally ill," he said. He also cited various psychiatric authorities which described the pattern of a manic depressive disease and maintained that this was consistent with Adrian's behaviour since 1974.

Testifying for the prosecution, Dr Chee provided the court another perspective of Adrian's state of mind and said: "There is no evidence to show that he suffered from any psychiatric illness. He has been purposeful in his pursuits, patient in his planning and persuasive in his performance for personal power and pleasure." Rejecting Dr Wong's diagnosis of manic depressive illness, Dr Chee said Adrian's attitude to the goddess Kali was not a delusion but a normal cultural or religious belief. He thought it dangerous to say Adrian's belief in the goddess became a delusion when he crossed the boundary of reality and wanted to kill children. Adrian exploited religion for personal gain and this showed that he was in full control of himself and well organised.

Dr Wong considered Adrian's attempted suicide as a symptom of his illness, but Dr Chee disputed this, saying it ran against a symptom of manic depressive illness – fear of dying. Dr Chee also discounted Adrian's complaint while in prison that he had hallucinations of Kali. He said the hallucinations occurred at night and it was not uncommon for prisoners kept in isolation to hallucinate.

Dr Chee disagreed that Adrian's personality changed around the time he developed an interest in the occult and got to know Mui Choo. Adrian's irritability occurred mainly when he was in a so-called trance. "Throughout evidence in court, there were two aspects of Adrian Lim. One was

Adrian Lim whom Mui Choo and Kah Hong found to be nice, and the other was when he was in a so-called trance," noted Dr Chee. He said Adrian made use of his so-called trances to get his own way. It did not mean he was sick. In his opinion, Adrian did not undergo a personality change. Rather, there was a change in Adrian's social behaviour after he learnt and began to practise the occult. Dr Chee maintained that a change in social behaviour did not mean he was mentally ill. As for Adrian's tendency to dominate others, he said the evidence showed that Adrian was a bully and a coward. Dr Wong had seen a symptom in Adrian's increased sexual activity, but Dr Chee said this could have been the result of having more opportunities to have sex. Besides, Adrian indulged in sexual perversions, which was quite different from hypersexuality, he said. As for Adrian's insomnia, Dr Chee said a manic depressive patient would not realise that he could not sleep, and usually his close family members would have to report this to the doctor. In Adrian's case, he saw several doctors and complained of insomnia and took sedatives voluntarily.

TAN MUI CHOO

Consultant psychiatrist R. Nagulendran examined Mui Choo in March and April 1981, after her arrest and after reading her statements to the police. He found her rational and able to describe coherently what took place during the killings. His diagnosis was that Mui Choo had reactive depressive psychosis, an abnormality of the mind serious enough to impair her mental responsibility for her actions. He told the court that although Mui Choo knew that what she did was against the law, she committed the offences "under compulsion and the perceptual delusion that the ritual of consuming blood and child sacrifice was in keeping with her faith in the Hindu goddess Kali". At the time of the killings, Mui Choo's state of mind was also affected by her consumption of psychotropic drugs, the electric shock treatments and threats of psychological and physical assault by Adrian. Once no longer dominated by him after her arrest, Mui Choo was able to realise the magnitude of what she had done.

Dr Nagulendran said Mui Choo's illness was characterised by symptoms of severe depression, which suggested a break with reality triggered by severe stress. He cited several symptoms consistent with reactive depressive psychosis. They included Mui Choo's very low moods, persistent insomnia, suicidal thoughts, restlessness, tension and fear, chronic headaches and loss of appetite. He thought her mental illness started in 1975 in the form of reactive depression, after she was forced into prostitution. Her symptoms at the time were mainly her depressed mood and insomnia. Her next role as a nightclub stripper, in addition to being a prostitute by day, left her feeling tired. She was also being assaulted by Adrian. Her symptoms worsened and later, she accepted Adrian's suggestion that she was possessed. The belief that she was possessed soon grew into an obsession and reached a delusional state by 1979. This marked the start of her reactive depressive psychosis and new symptoms included her paranoid delusions, hallucinations, severe depression, suicidal thoughts, guilt feelings and sense of worthlessness.

Dr Nagulendran noted that Adrian's electric shock treatments left Mui Choo feeling weak and her mind would go blank. She found it difficult to think for herself and did as she was told. When Adrian told her it was time to kill children, she was confused. Dr Nagulendran said Mui Choo did not believe in killing children but she was subjected to repeated suggestions that she should take part in Adrian's plan. "Her state of mind at the time she committed her offences was that of one suffering from reactive depressive psychosis. As a result, she carried out her acts with total resignation and obeyed instructions blindly and unquestioningly. She lacked a sense of judgment and self-control," the psychiatrist told the court.

Dr Chee disagreed with Dr Nagulendran's assessment of Mui Choo's state of mind. He examined Mui Choo in March 1981, reviewed her case in November 1982 and again during the trial. He read observation notes about Mui Choo during her stay at the Changi women's prison, the statements of the three accused, Dr Nagulendran's report and the evidence produced in court. Dr Chee felt there was no evidence of reactive depressive psychosis preceded by reactive depression. He agreed that Adrian's threats and beatings and the electric shock treatment might have left Mui Choo feeling depressed, but pointed to other evidence which indicated that she was not suffering from reactive depression. He did not have the impression that Mui Choo had an unhappy married life. She had indicated that she was quite content with Adrian, who gave her nice clothes, cosmetics and whatever she needed. In the months before the child killings, she visited beauticians twice a week and took $14,000 for her slimming treatment. If she was depressed all that time, she would have become increasingly neglectful of her personal appearance, Dr Chee said. Mui Choo had told him that she put up with Adrian not because of the torture and abuse she suffered, but because of the good times she enjoyed. She also agreed that she underwent the electric shock treatments to cure her headaches, not to get rid of evil spirits in her. There was ample evidence, he said, that Mui Choo assisted Adrian actively in his deceptions, that she agreed to have Agnes killed, and that she suggested where to dump the girl's body.

Dr Chee's opinion was that there was no evidence that Mui Choo suffered from a reactive depressive psychosis. "She was active, showing interest in herself and in touch with reality," he said.

During cross-examination by Mr J. B. Jeyaretnam, Dr Chee admitted that he had unintentionally overlooked the fact that Mui Choo was subjected to electric shock treatments and had been assaulted by Adrian. He agreed with counsel that these were significant factors and that he had made a glaring omission. Despite that, Dr Chee stood by his view that Mui Choo was not mentally ill at the time of the child killings.

HOE KAH HONG

Dr Nagulendran also testified on Kah Hong's behalf. He told the court that at the time of the killings, she had schizophrenia that was severe enough to impair her mental responsibility for her acts. Kah Hong had schizophrenia long before she met Adrian, and initially suffered a primary delusion that her mother wanted to harm her and had cast an evil spell on her. Under Adrian's influence, Kah Hong's illness worsened rapidly to such an extent that she beat her mother and poured urine on her mother's head. Kah Hong became depressed after Adrian told her the evil spirit in her had jumped out and killed her husband, Benson Loh Ngak Hua. Kah Hong was warded for 45 days at Woodbridge Hospital, but Dr Nagulendran said she suffered a relapse after being discharged. He said she agreed with Adrian's plan to kill children because she now developed a secondary delusion that killing was good and approved by the goddess Kali.

Dr Nagulendran noted that after her arrest, Kah Hong was cheerful and did not seem to realise the seriousness of what she had done. She told him that at the time of Agnes' death, she felt angry, excited and frightened. She was angry because Adrian had told her that Agnes would grow up to be evil like Kah Hong's mother and cast spells on other people unless she was killed. She could not explain why she felt excited, but said she was frightened when Adrian applied his electric shock devices to Agnes, as it reminded her of the electric shocks she had received herself. She said she felt sorry when Adrian applied the electrical devices to Ghazali, but felt nothing after the boy's body had been taken away from the flat. Dr Nagulendran's view was that Kah Hong did not know that participating in the killings was morally wrong, but she knew that what she did was against the law.

Dr Nagulendran's diagnosis that Kah Hong was mentally ill at the time of the child killings contrasted with the views of Woodbridge Hospital psychiatrists who treated her during her long stay there and during her follow-up visits. Kah Hong had schizophrenia, but she recovered rapidly after she was admitted to the hospital. She stopped being suicidal, depressed and hostile towards her mother. She progressed well and was allowed weekends home before she was finally discharged in mid-1980. In the six months that followed, she returned for follow-up appointments and was found to be well. Even on 31 January 1981, a week after Agnes' death, Kah Hong was found to be generally well with no sign of an apparent relapse.

Former Woodbridge psychiatrist Kok Lee Peng told the court that she saw Kah Hong after she was admitted in May 1980. She diagnosed Kah Hong to have schizophrenia as well as psychotic depression brought on by a grief reaction to her husband's death. Kah Hong believed her in-laws wanted her to die and would harm her. She was aggressive and shouted early during her hospital stay but gradually improved and by the time of her discharge, showed no symptoms. Dr Kok said Kah Hong still had schizophrenia, but doctors who saw Kah Hong during her follow-up visits in the months following her discharge noted that she had no complaints and appeared well, even on 31 January 1981.

Dr Chee's view was that Kah Hong was not schizophrenic, but even if she had schizophrenia, she was in a state of remission at the time of the killings. If she had suffered a relapse, no doctor would have missed the symptoms during her follow-up visits right up to the time of the child killings. He felt that if she had experienced the delusions Dr Nagulendran described, and if they had been so severe as to affect her mental responsibility, they would also have affected her ability to work. Instead, Kah Hong held her job and she played an active role in abducting and killing the children and in disposing of the bodies. Dr Chee recalled that while attached to Woodbridge, Dr Nagulendran presented Kah Hong's case to a conference of psychiatrists and the opinion was divided fifty-fifty that she had schizophrenia. Dr Chee said that in February 1983, after he had examined Kah Hong and concluded that she did not have schizophrenia, he put his case to a conference and this time the psychiatrists were unanimous that she did not have the illness. Dr Nagulendran and Dr Kok were not present at the conference.

Dr Chee also said that a mentally ill person was more likely to resist suggestions and hypnosis than a normal person. He therefore disputed the contention that Kah Hong believed Adrian's suggestions because she was of unsound mind. If psychiatric patients could be controlled and manoeuvred by suggestions, then psychiatrists would be the first to use this method to treat them, he said. Dr Chee also did not accept that Kah Hong had a fixed delusion about the goddess Kali after Adrian told her that the goddess liked to kill. He questioned whether it was likely that Adrian could have convinced Mui Choo and Kah Hong and made them share his delusion about Kali. If the defence case was that all three accused were mentally ill, Dr Chee found it difficult to believe how three people suffering from three different mental illnesses could possibly share the same delusion.

With Dr Chee's testimony, the trial drew to a close. Counsel for the accused made their winding-up speeches, each asking the judges to find his client a victim of a serious mental illness and to therefore spare Adrian, Mui Choo and Kah Hong from the gallows.

Mr Howard Cashin criticised Dr Chee's evidence, accusing the psychiatrist of shutting his eyes to Adrian's symptoms of mental disease. Mr Cashin reiterated the defence position, that Adrian had a normal extrovert personality until he was initiated into the occult in the mid-1970s. He underwent a clear personality change which marked the start of his mental illness and led him to excessive religiosity beyond his control. Adrian began to harm people through trickery and deceit, he had a persecution complex and was a master of deception. He became increasingly hypersexual and perverted, and at the same time, suffered his delusion about the goddess Kali and his desire to kill children for Kali. He manipulated his women into prostitution and lived off their earnings. Another symptom of his mental illness was his grandiosity – he had wealth and power over others, but wanted more. Mr Cashin maintained that Adrian made a clear break from reality when he entered the "unreasonable world of atrociousness" which culminated with the child killings.

Mr Jeyaretnam said Mui Choo had been depressed since 1975 and her condition worsened until, at the time of the child killings, her depression had become psychotic. Mui Choo's mental abnormality was reflected in her low moods, depression, the slowing down of her thinking, her inability to exercise willpower to control her actions; and her beliefs that she was possessed, that Adrian had supernatural powers and that the goddess Kali wanted child sacrifices. Mr Jeyaretnam said there was no disputing that Mui Choo participated in the killings, but the question was whether she planned the killings with Adrian and Kah Hong. His case was that Mui Choo acted throughout in a mechanical fashion, like a robot. Over the years, because of the stress and fear of living with Adrian, Mui Choo had been reduced to a state where she lacked the ability to exercise any willpower to resist him.

Mr Nathan Isaac put to the court that Kah Hong was insane at the time of the killings. If the judges did not accept that, his case was that she had schizophrenia and that impaired her mental responsibility for her actions. "Her schizophrenic mind accepted the idea that if the children were killed, they would go to heaven and not grow up evil like her mother and others. This is in keeping with her primary delusion of being paranoid towards her mother," he said. Mr Isaac criticised Dr Chee for failing to accept the symptoms Kah Hong presented as signs of her schizophrenia.

*

DPP Glenn Knight did not mince his words when he asked the judges to reject the defence claim that the three accused were victims of severe mental illness and therefore not fully responsible for their actions. His case was that Agnes and Ghazali were killed in cold blood. He told the judges: "The children were killed in a most cruel fashion for which there is no excuse in law or in fact. I would ask whether it is conceivable that three persons, like the three accused, suffering from three major mental illnesses and sharing the same delusion, could perpetrate these killings and carry them out in the manner they did and dispose of the bodies and the evidence. Should they not have faltered? The other most singularly unexplainable fact is that if it was the goddess Kali who motivated the killings, none of them should have told this to the police. Not Adrian, not Mui Choo, not Kah Hong. Yet in this court all three insist that they were deluding and had killed because of Kali. The fact that they did not mention this is suggestive of the fact that they were in control right up to the time of their arrest and were not suffering from the illnesses alleged. Even if there was the abnormality of mind, it could not have substantially impaired their responsibilities. The killings were for selfish motives."

Mr Knight said the evidence showed that the murders were the result of Adrian's anger at being accused of rape. Adrian decided to vent his anger at the police and persuaded Mui Choo and Kah Hong to go along with the idea. They planned how to lure children to the Toa Payoh flat and were cool and calculating in carrying out the murders and disposing of the bodies. Pressing for a deterrent sentence, he said: "The law on murder would be seriously undermined if its failure to act as a deterrent in this case is used as grounds to prove an abnormality of mind. It has been conceded that this is a unique case. The approach of the defence seems to be that because these killings are unique, unusual and do not represent the accepted thinking on the subject, they therefore arise from a delusion and that this is unlikely to happen again. My Lords, if the accused are not found guilty of murder because it is accepted that they killed for this reason, it will no longer be unique because others will do it."

Mr Knight said the evidence showed that Adrian was a selfish and cruel man who would stop at nothing. He was prepared to kill two children simply to distract the police from investigating the rape charges against him, and at the same time satisfy his desire to sexually assault a child. "His acts were perpetrated with cunning and deliberation. This is not a man who was under delusions about goddess Kali … Commonsense would suggest that neither he nor they [Mui Choo and Kah Hong] could let Agnes live after he had sexually mutilated her. How would he survive the ignominy of raping not only a woman, but also a child? Agnes had to be killed and killed she was. My Lords, to say that Adrian was less than a coward who preyed on little children because they could not fight back; and killed them in the hope that he would gain power or wealth by ritual worship and therefore did not commit murder, makes no sense of the law of murder. To lend credence to the shroud of mystery and magic he has conjured up by his practices to frighten, intimidate and persuade the superstitious, the weak and the gullible into participating in the most lewd and obscene acts is unacceptable. This court must expose that. To give effect to Adrian's defence is to lend credence to the myths of medicine men, *bomoh*s and mediums and their so-called magical powers."

Mr Knight maintained that Mui Choo did what she did in the child killings because she loved Adrian and not because she was an unwilling pawn, a gullible person or someone suffering from mental illness. As for Kah Hong, he felt that here was someone who had been misled, not someone with a mental illness.

CHAPTER 14

THE VERDICT

Justice T. S. Sinnathuray and Justice F. A.
Chua rejected the defence case that Adrian
Lim, Chua Mui Choo and Hoe Kah Hong
were suffering from serious mental illnesses
when they killed Agnes Ng Siew Heok and
Ghazali Marzuki. All three were found guilty
of murder and sentenced to death by hanging.

25 May 1983: In the days before smartphones, text messaging
and tweets, if you wanted to be among the first to hear the
news, you had to be at the scene. People curious to hear the
outcome of Singapore's most sensational "ritual killings" case
crowded the Supreme Court building from morning, even
though the verdict was not expected till afternoon. There was
limited seating in the public gallery of Courtroom No. 4 and
entry was on a first-come-first-served basis. Once all seats
were taken, the police encouraged the crowd to go home, but
nobody budged. By 2.30 p.m., when Justice Sinnathuray was

expected to deliver the judgment, hundreds had gathered outside the court building. Without a doubt, the bets were on among several of the faces in the crowd: Would all three hang, would Adrian alone hang, would at least one of the women escape death? They watched and waited, contained behind a police cordon.

Justice Sinnathuray took 15 minutes to deliver the verdict. A newspaper report described Adrian as appearing alert in the dock, smiling frequently and nodding at those in the courtroom, but listening intently as sentence was passed. Mui Choo and Kah Hong sat with their heads bowed, their hands folded on their laps.

Justice Sinnathuray and Justice Chua noted that Adrian, Mui Choo and Kah Hong had admitted the facts related to the child killings from the very outset. "Throughout the trial, the participation of each of them in furtherance of the common intention to kill the two children has never been in doubt. All these are found in the lengthy statements voluntarily given by the three of them to the police soon after their arrest," Justice Sinnathuray said. "The only defence of the three accused is that at the time of the commission of the offence each of them was suffering from diminished responsibility as defined in Exception 7 to Section 300 of the Penal Code. Accordingly, it is submitted that the three of them are guilty not of murder but of culpable homicide not amounting to murder. There is, however, one exception. On behalf of the third accused [Kah Hong], it is also submitted that we should consider the defence of insanity under Section

84 of the Penal Code. We have done so and we reject this latter submission as without foundation."

Exception 7 to Section 300 reads as follows: "Culpable homicide is not murder if the offender was suffering from such abnormality of mind (whether arising from a condition of arrested or retarded development of mind or any inherent causes or induced by disease or injury) as substantially impaired his mental responsibility for his acts and omissions in causing the death or being a party to causing the death." The judges said it was for the defence to prove that an accused person fell within these bounds. In the context of the evidence given at the trial, each accused would have to show that (a) he or she was suffering from an abnormality of mind induced by disease and (b) that the abnormality of mind was such that it substantially impaired his or her mental responsibility for the killing of the two children.

The judges said: "We have carefully considered, not just the medical evidence of each of the three accused and the evidence in rebuttal of them by the prosecution but, as we must as judges of facts, all the evidence before us. Now we have reviewed the whole of the evidence in the light of the submissions made to us by counsel for the defence and the prosecution. The decisions we have come to are these:

ADRIAN LIM

"As regards the first accused, we accept the opinions of Dr Chee Kuan Tsee and Dr R. Nagulendran that at the time of the commission of the two murders, the first

accused was not suffering from an abnormality of mind
induced by a disease of the mind – manic depressive illness
of the manic type. We are satisfied that at the material time,
the first accused was not suffering from any psychiatric
illness. From the evidence we find, as Dr Chee said, the
first accused was 'purposeful in his pursuits, patient in his
planning and persuasive in his performance for personal
power and pleasure'. We are revulsed by his abominable
and depraved conduct."

TAN MUI CHOO

"Next, as regards the second accused, we find that there is
evidence that when she lived with the first accused, there
were occasions when she suffered from depression. But on
a balance of probabilities, we find that at the time when the
second accused took part in the two murders, she was not
suffering from reactive depressive psychosis. That which
weighs heavily in our minds is that we had the benefit of
hearing and seeing her give evidence in the witness box.
The opinion we have of her is that she is an artful and
wicked person. In conspiracy with the first accused, she was
at all times a willing party to his loathsome and nefarious
acts. We have also considered her case on the footing that
she was suffering from the mental disease postulated by
Dr Nagulendran. Even if she was suffering from abnormality
of mind, we find that the abnormality was not such as
substantially impaired her mental responsibility for her acts
in the two killings."

HOE KAH HONG

"In contrast to the second accused, the third accused is a simple person who can be easily influenced. It is claimed that the third accused is suffering from schizophrenia. That diagnosis, however, is in issue between the psychiatrists. On the evidence before us, it appears that there are grounds for the disagreement. However, what comes out clearly in the evidence is that since her discharge from Woodbridge Hospital, some six months before the commission of the offences, she was thereafter at all times in a state of remission. We accordingly have no difficulty in finding that even if the third accused had suffered from schizophrenia, at the time of the commission of the offences she was not suffering from an abnormality of mind as substantially impaired her mental responsibility for the two killings."

With that, Adrian, Mui Choo and Kah Hong were found guilty and convicted of murdering Agnes and Ghazali, and sentenced to death. A newspaper report said the two women looked despondent but remained expressionless. Adrian, on the other hand, smiled broadly, nodded his head in approval and looked at Mui Choo and Kah Hong. As the three were about to be led away, Adrian called out to the judges: "Thank you, my Lords."

Before announcing their decision, the judges thanked those who had helped them during the 41-day trial: DPP Glenn Knight and his assistant Mr Roy Neighbour for their careful presentation of the prosecution case; and defence lawyers

Mr Howard Cashin and his assistant Mr Choo Han Teck, Mr J.B. Jeyaretnam and Mr Nathan Isaac. "They can take satisfaction that they have discharged their public duty courageously and, in the highest traditions of the Bar, they have given their best for their respective clients," Justice Sinnathuray said. The judges also paid tribute to the police team from the Criminal Investigation Department's Special Investigation Section, commending Inspector Richard Pereira for finding the killers soon after Ghazali's death, and Inspector Simon Suppiah for the diligence and thoroughness shown in the investigations.

Outside the Supreme Court building, news of the verdict spread quickly, but the crowd of hundreds still did not disperse. They stayed, hoping to catch a glimpse of the condemned trio as they were taken away to start their time on death row. It was about 3.15 p.m. when the three blue vans drove out of the court building. The crowd booed.

Mui Choo and Kah Hong appealed against their convictions, but Adrian declined the option, requesting instead to be hanged immediately. However, he had to wait until the women exhausted all avenues of having their conviction and death sentence overturned. Their first stop was the Court of Criminal Appeal in Singapore. Mui Choo engaged Mr Francis Seow, a former Solicitor General, to fight her appeal, while Kah Hong had Mr Nathan Isaac assigned as her counsel again. As at the trial, counsel hoped the appeal judges would find that the two women were suffering from major mental illnesses at the time of the child killings.

Their appeals were heard in November 1985 by Chief Justice Wee Chong Jin, Mr Justice Lai Kew Chai and Mr Justice L.P. Thean. In August 1986, the judges announced their decision: the women's appeals were dismissed. Recalling the deaths of the two children as well as Kah Hong's husband, Benson Loh Ngak Hua, the judges said: "The bizarre circumstances under which three people lost their lives deeply involved Adrian Lim, a pervert and an evil charlatan who studied and learnt occult practices to prey upon women and others who were in distress and who were therefore superstitiously vulnerable." The judges noted that Mui Choo supported Adrian with her earnings from prostitution, and assisted him in his work as a medium. Together they preyed on the gullible, and Adrian had even deceived Mui Choo into believing that he needed sex with young women to stay alive. In all their extraordinary activities, Mui Choo cooperated with Adrian and gave him active assistance. "Several girls fell prey to their evil devices as a result of which Adrian Lim indulged himself sexually and both of them gained financially," the judges said. As for Kah Hong, the judges upheld that she was in a state of remission from schizophrenia when she abducted Agnes and Ghazali, she knew what was going on throughout the two child killings and actively took part in getting rid of the bodies.

The two women subsequently appealed to the Privy Council in London and failed again. They exhausted their last avenue of hope when they failed in a request for clemency from President Wee Kim Wee.

Early on the morning of 25 November 1988, Adrian Lim, Tan Mui Choo and Hoe Kah Hong were hanged at Changi Prison. Among those who witnessed the executions was Catholic priest Brian Doro, an Australian missionary with the Redemptorist order that runs the well-known Novena Church in Thomson Road and a pioneer of the Roman Catholic Prison Ministry. He had visited Mui Choo and Kah Hong during their years on death row. Adrian asked to see him only in the final days of his life. In an interview with *The Straits Times* a year later, after he received the Public Service Medal for his exemplary work with prisoners and drug addicts, Father Doro said he found Adrian to be a "rather friendly fellow". He revealed that Adrian made his confession and received the Catholic last rites before his death. "Three days before he was hanged, Adrian Lim asked me to give him absolution and Holy Communion," he said. Describing what he felt when he watched condemned prisoners hanged within touching distance, the priest said: "It is like sending a friend off on a trip."

After the hangings, *The Straits Times* reported that Adrian went smiling to the gallows and Mui Choo and Kah Hong were calm. They were served cakes and drinks before they took their last walk to face death. The three coffins were taken later that morning to the Roman Catholic Church of the Holy Family in Katong for a service and all three were cremated the same day at Mount Vernon Crematorium. Almost eight years after Singapore was shaken by the Toa Payoh child killings, the unholy trinity was no more.

CHAPTER 15

REPENTANCE ON DEATH ROW

Roman Catholic nun Sister Gerard
Fernandez visited countless prisoners over
35 years as a pioneer volunteer counsellor
with the Roman Catholic Prison Ministry.
She became a death row counsellor after
Tan Mui Choo was sentenced to hang. In
January 2016, Sister Gerard, 78, spoke to
Alan John about her experience counselling
Mui Choo and Kah Hong, and how they
prayed for Adrian Lim to repent before they
went to the gallows.

The child murders of 1981 shocked all of Singapore, but
hit home especially among the Good Shepherd sisters, a
community of Roman Catholic nuns who run schools, a
vocational centre for girls and a shelter for women. They
knew the first victim, Agnes Ng Siew Heok, whose family
were devout Catholics. And when the police arrested three

people for killing Agnes and Ghazali Marzuki, the sisters were distressed to learn that one of the suspects was Tan Mui Choo, who had attended their Marymount Vocational Centre and whom they knew by her baptism name, Catherine.

No one was more disturbed than Sister Gerard Fernandez. "I knew Catherine, she was one of our girls. She came from a Catholic family, her parents were very religious, and we knew them too," she recalled. Sister Gerard was aware that the young woman had fallen into bad company after leaving the vocational centre. As the sensational case unfolded before the courts, she also knew of all the terrible details that emerged, including how Catherine's younger sister and brother had also been tricked by Adrian Lim.

When Adrian, Catherine and Hoe Kah Hong were sentenced to hang on 23 May 1983, Sister Gerard felt she had to act quickly. "I thought they were all going to hang the very next day!" she said. Some years earlier, in 1977, she had joined Redemptorist priests Father Brian Doro and Father Patrick John O'Neill in starting the Roman Catholic Prison Ministry to visit detained drug offenders and prisoners. She had never counselled anyone sentenced to hang, but now asked the director of prisons, Mr Quek Shi Lei, for permission to meet Catherine on death row.

"He gave me permission, but only if she was willing to meet me. He said, 'She must want to see you, and right now she doesn't want to see anybody.' So I wrote her a letter right away and I included a beautiful picture of Jesus. I think it touched her."

But Sister Gerard's letter went unanswered for six months. Then, out of the blue, a reply arrived one day from Catherine. Sister Gerard recalled: "Her first words to me were, 'Sister, how could you love me after what I have done?' And she signed her letter, 'Your black sheep, Catherine.' I immediately went and got permission to see her. It was the beginning of a period of healing for her."

That was how Sister Gerard began her weekly visits to Catherine, who was among a number of condemned women criminals in Changi Prison. The nun had been mistaken in thinking the trio's hangings were imminent. In fact, all three remained on death row for almost seven years until the women exhausted all avenues of appeal, and were executed on the same day in November 1988. Sister Gerard would go to Catherine's cell each week and stay half an hour, although she was not allowed to enter the cell. They would hold hands and chat, pray and sing hymns together.

One day, Catherine asked to make her confession, which is when Catholics tell a priest their sins, express sorrow and ask for forgiveness. "After that, her life changed," Sister Gerard said. "Catherine spent hours in prayer, and looked forward to the times when Father Doro would come and say the Mass in front of her cell with me, and she received the Eucharist."

Catherine's family had been devastated by her arrest, the courtroom revelations and her death sentence. She had been estranged from her parents, and was closer to her grandmother. Sister Gerard recalled that it took some time to persuade Catherine's father to visit her in prison. "I spoke to him and said look, she's done wrong, but she is still your daughter." He eventually came round. "He went to see her, and there was a moment of forgiveness," Sister Gerard said. That meeting took place just in time, because not long after, Catherine's father had a stroke and he died before she was hanged. Her mother visited her in prison and attended Father Doro's masses too. Sister Gerard said she saw a real change in Catherine over the years. Initially sad, upset and full of guilt, she gradually returned to her Catholic faith. "Once she was able to see that she had done wrong and admit it, and know that God forgave her, she was able to let go," she said. "She drew strength from God coming back into her life. Catherine was a lovely person, always happy and nice to all the prison wardens."

Like all death row prisoners, Catherine was in solitary confinement. Kah Hong occupied the cell next to hers. At first Sister Gerard visited Catherine only, though they were aware that from her cell, Kah Hong would listen intently to everything they said. "Later, Kah Hong asked to see me too, and I started visiting her as well." Kah Hong eventually asked to be baptised a Catholic and she took the name Geraldine, after the nun who visited her on death row.

The women's block was separate from the men's block where Adrian was held. Sister Gerard said the two women spoke to her about the time they were with Adrian. "They made a mistake," she says simply. "They were frightened of him. He used the electric shocks on them and they could not get away and they did not know what they were doing. But they were aware that they had done wrong. He was also a medium and he used that to fool them into doing a lot of things." Sister Gerard believes Satan exists in the world and is able to get a hold on individuals who are not careful. Adrian, who had been raised Catholic, had a choice. "We have a power within us and we can use it for evil or for good. He just chose to do evil," she said.

Asked if the two women forgave Adrian for all he had done and how he had led them to death row, Sister Gerard said: "It took some time, but they did." She had raised the subject, asking how they would feel when all three were led to the gallows, and Adrian would be there alongside them. "I asked them, would you be able to forgive him? They said yes. And then they began to pray for his conversion. About a week before the executions, Catherine, Kah Hong, Father Doro and I were singing Amazing Grace and praying at their cells, and they were saying to God, 'This is the last week of his life, do not let Adrian go without him asking for forgiveness.'"

Sister Gerard said the men and women's blocks were close enough for the male prisoners to hear them singing, and Adrian would have known Catherine and Kah Hong were singing that day. During all the years that he was behind bars, Adrian had refused to see a counsellor. Father Doro was a familiar presence among the male prisoners, including those on death row, and had accompanied many a condemned man to the gallows, staying by their side to the very end. "The prisoners loved him," Sister Gerard said of the priest who died in 2015. "He had a beautiful sense of humour, and could make the prisoners laugh." Although Adrian would have seen Father Doro over the years, it was not until that final week before the executions that he asked to see the priest. He asked for confession and communion. Sister Gerard said: "God works marvels. Adrian chose to repent, and God is forgiving."

But why pray for a killer like Adrian, why hope that he would seek forgiveness for all the evil that he did? "If you ask me that," Sister Gerard said, "then you should ask me why I visit prisoners at all. We may condemn them, but God condemns no one." To those who question how she could spend her time helping criminals who have committed the most awful crimes, Sister Gerard said: "We believe in a God who loves us. There is no other reason." She believes it was God who led her and Father Doro to work on death row. "Our whole lives are about reaching out to people, especially the broken, giving them back their wholeness and their identity as children of God."

After 35 years of walking with prisoners, Sister Gerard said Catherine remained vivid in her memories for a number of reasons. "She was my first death row prisoner," she said. What was also unusual was that although prison counsellors almost never meet the families of victims, in this case she knew Agnes' family, as well as Catherine's family. Sister Gerard and Father Doro sent off Adrian, Mui Choo and Kah Hong on the day they were hanged. Father Doro officiated and Sister

Gerard assisted at the funeral mass, which was attended by Catherine and Kah Hong's mothers, some family members and Good Shepherd sisters. Sister Gerard and Father Doro also accompanied the caskets to the crematorium that day.

Sister Gerard joined the Good Shepherd sisters 60 years ago, at the age of 18. She taught at and helped to run the Marymount vocational centre, but her work with prisoners and especially those on death row was to become a defining part of her calling to be a nun. She said people cringe when she tells them how a prisoner sometimes says to her: "Sister, I love you very much!" But that has helped her understand and appreciate her gift as a nun and counsellor. "I have a capacity to give love and receive love." She has described this elsewhere, saying: "While I abhor the death penalty, the taking of a life, I realise God's call to me to walk with these vulnerable people is for me to remember that 'He loved us first,' and allow them to experience healing and forgiveness through my love for them. They are precious moments when a man who has committed murder says to me the day before he is hanged, 'Don't worry Sister. I know God loves me! Tomorrow morning I will see Him face-to-face.'" For Sister Gerard, accompanying prisoners through the hardest times of their life means living up to the words of the foundress of her order, St Mary Euphrasia, who said: "One person is more precious than the whole world."

AUTHOR'S NOTE

Hindus regard Kali as the goddess of destruction. She is sometimes depicted as a fearsome multi-handed figure with long, dishevelled hair, wearing a belt of lopped-off human hands and a garland of human heads or skulls. In one hand, she holds a human head, dripping blood, and in another, a cleaver. Kali worshippers in the past have been said to make blood offerings to the goddess. There have been reports, especially from remote parts of India, of human sacrifices too. That, however, is not the norm. To most Hindus, Kali is regarded as the destroyer of evil and a goddess to turn to for help to avoid calamity. Pregnant women, for example, seek her help for a safe pregnancy and easy delivery. It is also not the norm for Hindus to smear blood on pictures or statues of the deities, or to drink blood.

ABOUT THE AUTHOR

Alan John was born in Kuala Lumpur in 1953 and attended St John's Institution and the University of Malaya before starting as a reporter at *The New Straits Times* in 1976. He moved to Singapore in 1980 and was a copyeditor at the paper's news desk when the Toa Payoh child murders happened in 1981. He spent 35 years at *The Straits Times*, heading various sections before becoming deputy editor, the position he held when he left in 2015. All the author's royalties from the 1989 edition of *Unholy Trinity* went to the Samaritans of Singapore. All royalties from the 2016 edition will go to Pave, Singapore's lead agency working with victims and perpetrators of family violence.